PRENTICE HALL
WRITING AND GRAMMAR

Reading Support Practice Book

Grade Twelve

Boston, Massachusetts,
Upper Saddle River, New Jersey

ISBN 0-13-361703-3

1 2 3 4 5 6 7 8 9 10   10 09 08 07 06

CONTENTS

Read the following passage. Then answer the questions that follow. Write the letter of the correct answer on the line at the right.

> There are photographs of my mother at this time, taken with three or four other girls, linked arm in arm or with their arms thrown jestingly around each other's necks. Behind them, beyond the sea or the hills or whatever is in the background, is a world already hurtling towards ruin, unknown to them: the theory of relativity has been discovered, acid is accumulating at the roots of trees, the bull-frogs are doomed. But they smile with something that from this distance you could almost call gallantry, their right legs thrust forward in parody of a chorus line.

[Margaret Atwood, "Significant Moments in the Life of My Mother"]

1. What inference can you make about the narrator's outlook toward the girls in the photographs?
   A. The girls deserve praise for their effort and hard work.
   B. The girls should have prepared more thoroughly for the photograph session.
   C. The girls secretly dislike one another.
   D. The girls are naive about the world's changing realities.   1. ______

2. Which sentence gives the main idea of the passage?   2. ______
   A. the first sentence   C. the third sentence
   B. the second sentence   D. the main idea is implied, not stated

3. Using context clues from the passage, you can define the word *gallantry* as   3. ______
   A. feminine intuition   C. heroic courage
   B. friendliness   D. appreciation

Read the following passage. Then answer the questions that follow. Write the letter of the correct answer on the line at the right.

> He was walking swiftly through the dark tunnel of foliage that in day-time was a road. The dogs were invisibly ranging the lower travelways of the bush, and he heard them panting. Sometimes he felt a cold muzzle on his leg before they were off again, scouting for a trail to follow. They were not trained, but free-running companions of the hunt, who often tired of the long stalk before the final shots, and went off on their own pleasure. Soon he could see them, small and wild-looking in a wild strange light, now that the bush stood trembling on the verge of color, waiting for the sun to paint earth and grass afresh.

[Doris Lessing, "A Sunrise on the Veld"]

4. At first, why can't the character in the passage see the dogs?   4. ______
   A. It is too dark out.   C. The dogs are too fast.
   B. The dogs are not trained.   D. The dogs are too far away.

5. From context clues in the passage, how would you define *stalk*?   5. ______
   A. careful pursuit   C. stem of a flower
   B. limping walk   D. loud bark

6. Why does the writer refer to the sun as painting the earth and the grass?   6. ______
   A. The phrase is used metaphorically to describe sunrise.
   B. The atmosphere is particularly hazy.
   C. The phrase refers to the sun god, who is portrayed as a painter in the
      mythology of some African peoples.
   D. The desert landscape is monotonous.

7. This excerpt suggests that the writer's overall purpose in the selection is   7. ______
   A. to inform   C. to entertain
   B. to persuade   D. to praise

Read the following passage. Then answer the questions that follow. Write the letter
of the correct answer on the line at the right.

> There was nothing he couldn't do, nothing! A vision came to him, as he stood
> there, like when a child hears the word "eternity" and tries to understand it,
> and time takes possession of the mind. He felt his life ahead of him as a great
> and wonderful thing, something that was his; and he said aloud, with the blood
> rising to his head: all the great men of the world have been as I am now, and
> there is nothing I can't become, nothing I can't do; there is no country in the
> world I cannot make part of myself, if I choose. I contain the world. I can make
> of it what I want. If I choose, I can change everything that is going to happen:
> it depends on me, and what I decide now.

[Doris Lessing, "A Sunrise on the Veld"]

8. Which of the following sentences is the best paraphrase for the second   8. ______
   sentence of the passage?
   A. He was very young when he had a vision of eternity.
   B. He was not used to experiencing visions of eternity.
   C. As he experienced the vision, he was like a child trying to understand
      eternity.
   D. Nothing was impossible for him, and he would live forever.

9. Based on this excerpt, what kind of judgment can you make about the   9. ______
   character in the passage?
   A. He is sensitive and easily hurt.
   B. He feels confident and in control of his own destiny.
   C. He is pessimistic about the future.
   D. He would like to move to another country.

Read the following passage. Then answer the questions that follow. Write the letter of the correct answer on the line at the right.

> My wife and I are not real farmers—not even Lerice, really. We bought our place, ten miles out of Johannesburg on one of the main roads, to change something in ourselves, I suppose; you seem to rattle about so much within a marriage like ours. You long to hear nothing but a deep, satisfying silence when you sound a marriage. The farm hasn't managed that for us, of course, but it has done other things, unexpected, illogical. Lerice, who I thought would retire there in Chekhovian sadness for a month or two, and then leave the place to the servants while she tried yet again to get a part she wanted and become the actress she would like to be, has sunk into the business of running the farm with all the serious intensity with which she once imbued the shadows in a playwright's mind. I should have given it up long ago if it had not been for her. Her hands, once small and plain and well-kept—she was not the sort of actress who wears red paint and diamond rings—are hard as a dog's pads.

[Nadine Gordimer, "Six Feet of the Country"]

10. Which of the following statements best expresses the problem that the couple 10. ______
    wanted to solve by buying the farm?
    A. They wanted to live more economically than they could in the city of
       Johannesburg.
    B. They wanted to preserve the land from industrial development.
    C. They wanted to live in a more healthful climate.
    D. They wanted to change something in themselves and in their marriage.

11. What conclusion can you draw about Lerice from the passage? 11. ______
    A. She is enthusiastic about running the farm.
    B. She longs to resume her career as an actress.
    C. She resents her husband for buying the farm.
    D. She misses city life but stays on the farm because of her husband.

12. Choose the meaning that best fits the way *sound* is used in the third sentence 12. ______
    of the passage.
    A. to ring or echo   C. to explore or probe
    B. a noise   D. firm and stable

13. Which of the following statements best summarizes the passage? 13. ______
    A. Unexpectedly, the narrator and his wife have benefited from buying the
       farm, even though they are not real farmers.
    B. The husband dislikes the farm, but the wife loves it.
    C. Life on the farm is a refreshing change from life in the city.
    D. Although the husband tries to please his wife, she is always discontented.

Read the following passage. Then answer the questions that follow. Write the letter of the correct answer on the line at the right.

> In the process of writing the anecdotes of the past, and recalling the emotions and pains of my fate, and telling part of the history of my country, I found that life became more comprehensible and the world more tolerable. I felt that my roots had been recovered and that during that patient exercise of daily writing I had also recovered my own soul. I felt at that time that writing was unavoidable—that I couldn't keep away from it. Writing is such a pleasure; it is always a private orgy, creating and recreating the world according to my own laws, fulfilling in those pages all my dreams and exorcising some of my demons.

[Isabel Allende, "Writing as an Act of Hope"]

14. Which sentence states the main idea of the passage? **14.** ______
    A. the first sentence   B. the third sentence
    B. the second sentence   C. the last sentence

15. When you are evaluating the author's opinion of writing, it would be helpful **15.** ______
    to keep in mind that
    A. the author is a professional writer
    B. the author is from a foreign country
    C. the author is a member of an opposition party
    D. the author has never discovered her own roots

16. This passage most likely is an excerpt from **16.** ______
    A. an informative essay   C. a comic drama
    B. a persuasive editorial   D. a textbook chapter

Read the following passage. Then answer the questions that follow. Write the letter of the correct answer on the line at the right.

> You will shortly be hearing of that new school of psychology…which after long and far-adventuring research and experiment has established that all of the young of the human species are born omniscient. Babies, in their waking hours, know everything that is going on everywhere in the world; they can tune in to any conversation they choose, switch on to any scene. We have all experienced this power. It is only after the first year that it was brainwashed out of us; for it is demanded of us by our immediate environment that we grow to be of use to it in a practical way. Gradually, our know-all brain-cells are blacked out, although traces remain in some individuals in the form of E.S.P., and in the adults of some primitive tribes.
>
> It is not a new theory. Poets and philosophers, as usual, have been there first. But scientific proof is now ready and to hand. Perhaps the final touches are being put to the new manifesto in some cell at Harvard University. Any day now it will be given to the world, and the world will be convinced.

[Muriel Spark, "The First Year of My Life"]

17. In this passage, the writer humorously presents a nonfact as a fact. Which   17. ______
    statement best expresses this nonfact?
    A. Babies know everything that goes on everywhere.
    B. Babies make use of E.S.P. at night.
    C. A new school of psychology has picked up where poets and philosophers
       left off.
    D. Babies have some surprising similarities to adults.

18. Some information in the selection is important and some is unimportant. Choose   18. ______
    the statement below that is not important to the main idea of the passage.
    A. The young of the human species are born omniscient.
    B. Babies can tune in to any conversation they choose.
    C. After the first year, babies gradually lose their know-all brain-cells.
    D. A group at Harvard University may be putting the finishing touches on the
       new theory.

Read the following passage. Then answer the questions that follow. Write the letter
of the correct answer on the line at the right.

> She called them the paintbox houses because there was something about them
> that reminded her of a child's drawing and because each had its front door
> painted a different color, yellow, red, blue, lime, orange, and chocolate.
>
> "It's called Paragon Place," said Mrs. Upton, her cleaner and general help,
> when the building was completed.
>
> "What a ridiculous name! Paintbox Place would be far more suitable."
>
> Mrs. Upton ignored this as she ignored all of Avice Julian's remarks which she
> regarded as "showing off," affected, or just plain senile.
>
> "They do say," she said, "that the next thing'll be they'll start building on that
> bit of waste ground next door."
>
> "Waste ground?" said Mrs. Julian distantly. "Can you possibly mean the wood?"
>
> "Waste ground" had certainly been a misnomer, though "wood" was an exag-
> geration. It was a couple of rustic acres, more or less covered with trees....

[Ruth Rendell, "Paintbox Place"]

19. On the basis of the dialogue, which statement best expresses the contrast   19. ______
    between Mrs. Upton and Mrs. Julian?
    A. Mrs. Upton is polite, while Mrs. Julian is abrupt.
    B. Mrs. Upton is practical, while Mrs. Julian is imaginative.
    C. Mrs. Upton is orderly, while Mrs. Julian is disorganized.
    D. Mrs. Upton is generous, while Mrs. Julian is selfish.

20. As used in the passage, the word *waste* means   20. ______
    A. wild or uncultivated   C. left over
    B. ruined   D. vast

Read the following passage. Then answer the questions that follow. Write the letter of the correct answer on the line at the right.

At night his antelope skin was spread where the darkness overtook him—sometimes in a Sunnyasi monastery by the roadside; sometimes by a mud pillar shrine of Kala Pir, where the Jogis, who are another misty division of holy men, would receive him as they do those who know what castes and divisions are worth; sometimes on the outskirts of a little Hindu village, where the children would steal up with the food their parents had prepared; and sometimes on the pitch of the bare grazing-grounds where the flame of his stick-fire waked the drowsy camels. It was all one to Purun Das—or Purun Bhagat, as he called himself now. Earth, people, and food were all one. But, unconsciously, his feet drew him northward and eastward; from the south to Rohtak; from Rohtak to Kurnool; from Kurnool to ruined Samanah, and then upstream along the dried bed of the Gugger river that fills only when the rain falls in the hills, till, one day, he saw the far line of the great Himalayas.

[Rudyard Kipling, "The Miracle of Purun Bhagat"]

21. How is the direction of Purun Bhagat's journey toward the Himalayas described?   21. ______
    A. southward   **C.** northward and eastward
    B. downstream on the Gugger   **D.** above the grazing-grounds

22. What generalization can you make about the country where this story is set?   22. ______
    A. The country is poor, but its inhabitants are hospitable.
    B. Thriving cities dot the countryside.
    C. The inhabitants of the countryside are selfish and materialistic.
    D. The countryside no longer interests Purun Bhagat.

23. Which sentence below best expresses one of the main ideas in this passage?   23. ______
    A. Earth, people, and food were all one.
    B. The bed of the Gugger fills only when the rain falls in the hills.
    C. The Jogis are a division of holy men.
    D. Children would steal up with the food their parents had prepared.

24. According to the passage, Purun Bhagat visited Kurnool   24. ______
    A. after he left Rohtak
    B. after he saw the far line of the Himalayas
    C. after he arrived at Samanah
    D. after he went upstream along the Gugger river bed

25. Which one of the following statements is not a valid inference from the passage?   25. ______
    A. Purun Bhagat has adopted a life of poverty.
    B. Purun Bhagat is unconsciously attracted to the region of the Himalayas.
    C. Many people fail to recognize Purun Bhagat as a person who has dedicated himself to wisdom and saintliness.
    D. The Himalayas may be the setting for the next important episode in the story.

Read the following passage. Then answer the questions that follow. Write the letter of the correct answer on the line at the right.

> Then the people ran as only hill folk can run, for they knew that in a landslip you must climb to the highest ground across the valley. They fled, splashing through the little river at the bottom, and panted up the terraced fields on the far side, while the Bhagat and his brethren followed. Up and up the opposite mountain they climbed, calling to each other by name—the roll-call of the village—and at their heels toiled the big *barasingh,* weighted by the failing strength of Purun Bhagat. At last the deer stopped in the shadow of a deep pine-wood, five hundred feet up the hillside. His instinct, that had warned him of the coming slide, told him he would be safe here.

[Rudyard Kipling, "The Miracle of Purun Bhagat"]

26. In what direction did the hill folk run?　　　　　　　　　　26. _______
    A. across the valley and up the opposite mountain
    B. along the river at the bottom of the valley
    C. southward down the mountain
    D. eastward toward the rising sun

27. From context clues in the passage, a *barasingh* is a type of　　27. _______
    A. lion   **C.** horse
    B. goat   **D.** deer

28. Why does the *barasingh* stop at a point five hundred feet up the hillside?　　28. _______
    A. Purun Bhagat is too heavy for him to carry any farther.
    B. His instinct warns him of another landslide.
    C. His instinct tells him he will be safe.
    D. He wants to rest in the shade of the pine-wood.

Read the following passage. Then answer the questions that follow. Write the letter of the correct answer on the line at the right.

> A shoemaker named Simon, who had neither house nor land of his own, lived with his wife and children in a peasant's hut and earned his living by his work. Work was cheap but bread was dear, and what he earned he spent for food. The man and his wife had but one sheepskin coat between them for winter wear, and even that was worn to tatters, and this was the second year he had been wanting to buy sheepskins for a new coat.

[Leo Tolstoy, "What Men Live By"]

29. Which statement best expresses the implied main idea of the passage?　　29. _______
    A. Simon and his family are very poor.
    B. Winter is approaching.
    C. Simon makes his living as a shoemaker.
    D. The single coat the couple owns is in tatters.

　　　　　　　　　　　　　　　　Pretest   **7**

30. Which word below is closest to the meaning of the word *dear* in the second sentence?   **30.** ______
    A. affectionate   C. cherished
    B. expensive   D. tender

Read the following passage. Then answer the questions that follow. Write the letter of the correct answer on the line at the right.

> More completely than most writers, perhaps, Dickens can be explained in terms of his social origin, though actually his family history is not quite what one would infer from his novels. His father was a clerk in government service, and through his mother's family he had connections with both the army and the navy. But from the age of nine onwards he was brought up in London in commercial surroundings, and generally in an atmosphere of struggling poverty….If one wants a modern equivalent, the nearest would be H. G. Wells, who has had a rather similar history and who obviously owes something to Dickens as a novelist.

[George Orwell, "Charles Dickens"]

31. Which of the following statements is a fact presented in the selection?   **31.** ______
    A. Dickens began to write novels as a child.
    B. The family of Dickens's mother had connections with the army and the navy.
    C. Dickens and H. G. Wells wrote the same kinds of novels.
    D. Dickens grew up in comfortable surroundings.

32. Which of the following statements is an opinion presented in the selection?   **32.** ______
    A. Dickens's father was a clerk in government service.
    B. Dickens was brought up in London from the age of nine onwards.
    C. Dickens can be explained in terms of his social origin.
    D. The novels of Dickens have remained extremely popular.

33. Which of the following sources do you think the writer may have used for the information about Dickens's parents?   **33.** ______
    A. an encyclopedia or a biography of Dickens
    B. a dictionary
    C. an almanac
    D a magazine article

34. The statement that H. G. Wells owes something to Dickens as a novelist may be regarded as   **34.** ______
    A. a fact   C. a paraphrase
    B. an opinion   D. a nonfact

Read the following passage. Then answer the questions that follow. Write the letter of the correct answer on the line at the right.

> A wave of yet more tender joy escaped from his heart and went coursing in warm flood along his arteries. Like the tender fires of stars moments of their life together, that no one knew of or would ever know of, broke upon and illumined his memory. He longed to recall to her those moments, to make her forget the years of their dull existence together and remember only their months of ecstasy. For the years, he felt, had not quenched his soul or hers. Their children, his writing, her household cares had not quenched all their souls' tender fire. In one letter he had written to her then he had said: *Why is it that words like these seem to me so dull and cold? Is it because there is no word tender enough to be your name?*

[James Joyce, "The Dead"]

35. In the first sentence, what figure of speech does the writer use to compare joy to a wave?   35. _______
    A. simile   C. personification
    B. metaphor   D. paradox

36. Which of the following connotations are suggested by the word *illumined* at the end of the second sentence?   36. _______
    A. insight and warmth   C. inflammation and pain
    B. anguish and fear   D. doubt and hesitation

37. Which of the following statements best expresses the main idea of this passage?   37. _______
    A. The man's writing has endangered the couple's marriage.
    B. The man is dissatisfied with his writing.
    C. The man feels that he and his wife are still passionately in love.
    D. The man wants to write another letter to his wife.

38. Which of the inferences below is best supported by the evidence in the passage?   38. _______
    A. The story takes place in the nineteenth century.
    B. The couple has had moments of great happiness together, but also longer stretches of dull existence.
    C. The man wants to change careers.
    D. The wife has been an excellent mother to the children.

39. What problem does the man confront in the passage?   39. _______
    A. He wonders how to improve his writing.
    B. He struggles to remember the good times in his marriage and to forget the bad.
    C. He wonders how to remind his wife of the moments of ecstasy they have shared in the past.
    D. He wonders how to interest the children in his writing.

Read the following passage. Then answer the questions that follow. Write the letter of the correct answer on the line at the right.

> Her time was running out but she continued to sit by the window, leaning her head against the window curtain, inhaling the odor of dusty cretonne. Down far in the avenue she could hear a street organ playing. She knew the air. Strange that it should come that very night to remind her of the promise to her mother, her promise to keep the home together as long as she could. She remembered the last night of her mother's illness; she was again in the close dark room at the other side of the hall and outside she heard a melancholy air of Italy.

[James Joyce, "Eveline"]

40. Which of the following judgments about the overall tone of the passage do you think is most accurate?   40. ______
   A. cheerful   C. sad
   B. angry   D. suspenseful

41. Which item below is the best definition of the word *air* as it is used in the passage?   41. ______
   A. breeze   C. atmosphere
   B. musical tune   D. to publicize

42. When did the daughter make a promise to her mother?   42. ______
   A. during her mother's last illness
   B. after the daughter returned from Italy
   C. when the daughter heard the organ grinder
   D. as the daughter sat by the window

43. Which of the following statements best summarizes the passage?   43. ______
   A. As she sat by the window, she remembered the promise she had made to her mother to keep the home together.
   B. As she sat by the window, she heard a street organ playing.
   C. She remembered that her mother had died in the room on the other side of the hall.
   D. She felt a wave of longing for Italy.

Use this chart to answer the questions that follow.

Geologic Era	Geologic Developments	Life Forms
Triassic: 230–195 million years ago	Climate warming; semiarid to arid; plates begin to break into continents	First dinosaurs; possible evolution of first mammals
Jurassic: 195–140 million years ago	North America and Africa separate; ocean basins open	Reptiles dominant; first bird appears
Cretaceous: 140–65 million years ago	South America and Africa separate; chalk deposits	Snakes, lizards, flowering plants

On the line at the right, write the letter of the correct answer.

44. ______

44. What are the dates of the Jurassic Era?
   A. 280–230 million years ago
   B. 230–195 million years ago
   C. 195–140 million years ago
   D. 140–65 million years ago

45. ______

45. All of the following are associated with the Triassic Era except
   A. warm climate and arid conditions
   B. the first dinosaurs
   C. the possible evolution of the first mammals
   D. the separation of South America from Africa

Read the following passage. Then answer the questions that follow. Write the letter of the correct answer on the line at the right.

> Everybody else said of her: "She is such a good mother. She adores her children." Only she herself, and her children themselves, knew it was not so. They read it in each other's eyes.
>
> There were a boy and two little girls. They lived in a pleasant house with a garden and they had discreet servants, and felt themselves superior to anyone in the neighborhood.
>
> Although they lived in style, they felt always an anxiety in the house. There was never enough money. The mother had a small income and the father had a small income, but not nearly enough for the social position which they had to keep up. The father went into town to some office. But though he had good prospects, these prospects never materialized. There was always the grinding sense of the shortage of money, though the style was always kept up.

[D. H. Lawrence, "The Rocking-Horse Winner"]

46. ______

46. Which of the following statements is the best paraphrase of the first paragraph?
   A. Although the mother pretended to love her children, she and the children knew this pretense was only a show.
   B. People who praised the mother formed their opinion of her too quickly.
   C. The children were disobedient, but their mother loved them anyway.
   D. It was difficult for the mother to love her three children equally.

47. ______

47. What conclusion can you draw from the passage about the father?
   A. He tries hard but is not successful at his work.
   B. He holds a nondescript job, and his hopes and plans never seem to be fulfilled.
   C. He loves his children dearly.
   D. He treats the servants well.

48. The main contrast that the passage emphasizes is   48. ______
   A. between the family's social pretensions and their lack of money to pay for them
   B. between the father's personality and the mother's
   C. between the children's attitudes toward their parents and the neighbors' attitudes
   D. between the father's background and the mother's

49. In the last sentence, what connotation would you associate with the word   49. ______
grinding?
   A. crushing   **C.** smoothing
   B. boring   **D.** sharpening

50. From the content of this passage, you can reliably infer that it comes from a   50. ______
   A. speech   **C.** letter
   B. magazine article   **D.** short story

CONTEXT CLUES

Introduction

When you come across an unfamiliar word, look for context clues to help you figure out its meaning. **Context clues** may be found in the words, phrases, and sentences that surround the unfamiliar word.

Types of Context Clues
- synonyms
- comparisons
- clues that provide a general sense of the word
- definitions
- explanations

Model 1

As you read this sentence from "The Lady in the Looking Glass: A Reflection" by Virginia Woolf, notice how the underlined context clues give the reader a general sense of the meaning of the word *transient*.

> Meanwhile, since all the doors and windows were open in the heat, there was a perpetual sighing and ceasing sound, the voice of the **transient** and the perishing, it seemed, coming and going like human breath, while in the looking glass things had ceased to breathe and lay still in the trance of immortality.

A careful reader might guess that the word *transient* has to do with being temporary and define *transient* as "passing through quickly."

Model 2

As you read this passage, look for a synonym of the word *superficial*.

> At once the looking glass began to pour over her a light that seemed to fix her; that seemed like some acid to bite off the unessential and **superficial** and to leave only the truth.

Were you able to guess the meaning? Something *superficial* is on the surface or shallow.

Model 3

In this passage, notice how a comparison helps define the word *prizing*.

> To talk of "**prizing** her open," as if she were an oyster, to use any but the finest and subtlest and most pliable tools upon her was impious and absurd.

How would you define *prizing* based on this comparison?

Model 4

A definition in this passage signals the meaning of the word *reticent*.

> Without making any thought precise—for she was one of those **reticent** people whose minds hold thoughts enmeshed in clouds of silence—she was filled with thoughts.

Practice
Part I

The passages that follow are from "The Distant Past" by William Trevor. On the lines provided, write context clues that help you define the underlined words. Then write a definition of each word. Check your definition in the dictionary.

> They had always been thin, silent with one another, and similar in appearance: a brother and sister who shared a family face. It was a bony countenance, with pale blue eyes and a sharp, well-shaped nose and high cheekbones.

1. Unknown word: countenance
   Context Clues:

   ____

   ____

   ____

   ____

   Definition:

   ____

   ____

> When he died, in 1924, his two children discovered that they possessed only a dozen acres. It was locally said also that this adversity hardened their will and that because of it they came to love Carraveagh more than they could ever have loved a husband or a wife.

2. Unknown word: adversity
   Context Clues:

   ____

   ____

   ____

   ____

   Definition:

   ____

   ____

Part II

The following passage is also from "The Distant Past" by William Trevor.
Read the passage. Then complete the chart on the next page.

> Fat Driscoll, with a farmer called Maguire and another called Breen, had stood in the hall of Carreveagh, each of them in charge of a shotgun. The Middletons, children then, had been locked with their mother and father and an aunt in an upstairs room. Nothing else had happened: the expected British soldiers had not, after all, arrived and the men in the hall had eventually relaxed their vigil. "A massacre they wanted," the Middletons' father said after they'd gone…."Bloody ruffians."
>
> The Second World War took place. Two Germans, a man and his wife called Winkelmann who ran a glove factory in the town, were suspected by the Middletons of being spies for the Third Reich. People laughed, for they knew the Winkelmanns well and could lend no credence to the Middletons' latest fantasy—typical of them, they explained to the Winkelmanns, who had been worried. Soon after the War the Reverend Packham died and was replaced by the Reverend Bradshaw, a younger man who laughed also and regarded the Middletons as an anachronism. They protested when prayers were no longer said for the Royal Family in St. Patrick's, but the Reverend Bradshaw considered that their protests were as absurd as the prayers themselves had been. Why pray for the monarchy of a neighboring island when their own island had its chosen President now?

NAME ____ **DATE** ___________

Unfamiliar Word	Context Clues	Definition
vigil		
ruffians		
credence		
anachronism		
monarchy		

CONNOTATION/DENOTATION

Introduction

Every word has an exact, specific meaning, or **denotation.** A word's denotation is its dictionary definition. The denotative meaning of a word does not necessarily have positive or negative feelings associated with it.

Sometimes a word also has one or more **connotations,** or shades of meaning that stem from attitudes or emotional meanings connected to the word. A word's connotations are usually either positive or negative.

Two words can have similar denotations, but their connotations can differ. Notice the difference in meaning between the words in italics in the following sentences:

Most of our classmates admire Rachel as a *proud* leader.

Rachel sometimes behaves, however, like a *haughty* leader.

The denotations, or dictionary meanings, of *proud* and *haughty* are similar. However, in the first sentence, the word *proud* has a positive connotation, while the word *haughty* in the second sentence has a negative connotation because it refers to someone who is arrogant or overly proud.

Read the following pairs of sentences. Note the differences in connotation between the words in italics.

The team played *boldly* in the last quarter.

The team played *recklessly* in the final quarter.

The denotations of *boldly* and *recklessly* both suggest a readiness to take risks. However, *recklessly* is usually used in a negative sense to indicate rashness or irresponsibility.

After the favorable review of the play appeared, Teresa felt *happy.*

After the favorable review of the play appeared, Teresa felt *ecstatic.*

Happy and *ecstatic* both denote pleasure or joy. However, *ecstatic* has strong positive connotations, suggesting that Teresa was overpowered by joy and delight.

Reading Tip

As you read, keep in mind that writers convey their judgments and feelings about a subject by the words they choose. Pay particular attention to the connotations of specific words. A writer who describes a character as scrawny, instead of slender, is inviting the reader to share an attitude.

NAME ____________________________   **DATE** ____________

Practice

Read the following passage from "Opening Statement for the Inaugural Session of the Forum for Peace and Reconciliation" by Judge Catherine McGuinness.

The Forum is inclusive in its nature; already it contains members from all of the island of Ireland. I very much hope that in the future other Parties and other individuals will feel able to join in our deliberations. The forum does not represent a threat to any section of the people of Ireland. As I have already said, participation in it is entirely without prejudice to the position on constitutional issues held by any Party. The only entry test is a commitment to "peaceful and democratic means."

This Forum is about people rather than about territory. It is about people's right to live peacefully on this island "which we love and for whose welfare we pray," as that courageous Presbyterian minister, James Armour of Ballymoney, once said.

A. Connotation/Denotation

In a dictionary, find the denotation of each of these general words, and write it in the second column of the chart. Then find a word in the passage that has a similar meaning. Write the word in the third column. In the fourth column, indicate whether the word from the passage has a positive or negative connotation.

General Word	Denotation	Related Word	Connotation
open			
discussions			
preconception			
pledge			
brave			

B. Challenge!

For each of these general words, write a word that has the same denotation. Label the new word positive or negative. Then use your words in sentences that express the connotations of the words.

1. move ____

2. talk ____

3. tall ____

4. smooth____

5. slow ____

MULTIPLE-MEANING WORDS

Introduction

Readers often encounter words with more than one meaning. To determine the sense in which such **multiple-meaning words** are used, it is necessary to look at the context in which they occur. A word's context is made up of the sentence in which it appears and/or the parts of the passage immediately surrounding it. By considering a multiple-meaning word's context, the reader can determine which meaning is appropriate.

Note the differences in the meaning of *tender* in the following sentences.

> Ms. Johnston's manner in the kindergarten class was always *tender* and supportive.
>
> Embarrassed by his rude behavior, Sam was eager to *tender* an apology.

In the first sentence, the meaning of *tender* as an adjective is "gentle; mild." In the second sentence, the word *tender* is a verb, meaning "offer; present for acceptance." Context clues help you determine the meaning of *tender* in each sentence.

Most dictionaries contain a numbered definition for each meaning of a word. For some words, such as *set,* there can be as many as twenty definitions. Sometimes a word with multiple meanings is pronounced differently, depending on the meaning; for example, *con´duct* as a noun and *con duct´* as a verb.

Study the multiple-meaning words shown on the chart below. Note how the context clues in each of the example sentences reveal the meaning of the word as it is being used.

Word	Meaning	Example
function	• to operate or be in working order • an elaborate social occasion	• The car brakes were too wet to *function* properly. • They spent days preparing for last night's *function*.
craft	• special skill or art • boat, ship, or aircraft	• I admired the sculptor's *craft*. • The steersman guided his *craft* skillfully into the harbor.
patient	• tolerant and calm • person receiving medical care or treatment	• Nan was always *patient* under stress. • That hospital *patient* is scheduled for surgery today.
console	• to comfort or make feel less sad • instrument panel or unit with gauges or controls	• I wrote a long letter to *console* Tonya after her loss. • The pilot checked the gauges on the *console*.

NAME _______________________ DATE _______

Practice

Read the following passage from "The Rights We Enjoy, the Duties We Owe" by Tony Blair.

> People need rules which we all stand by, fixed points of agreement which impose order on chaos. That does not mean a return to the old hierarchy of deference. That is at best nostalgia, at worst reactionary. We do not want old class structures back. We do not want women chained to the sink. We do not want birth rather than merit to become once again the basis of personal advancement. Nor does it mean bureaucracy and regulation. Bad and foolish rules are bad and foolish rules, but they do not invalidate the need to have rules.
>
> Duty is the cornerstone of a decent society. It recognizes more than self. It defines the context in which rights are given. It is personal; but it is also owed to society. Respect for others—responsibility to them—is an essential prerequisite of a strong and active community. It is the method through which we can build a society that does not subsume our individuality but allows it to develop healthily. It accords instinct with common sense. It draws on a broader and therefore more accurate notion of human nature than one formulated on insular self-interest. The rights we receive should reflect the duties we owe. With power should come responsibility.

A. Multiple-Meaning Words

Find five words in the passage that have more than one meaning. In the left column, write each word and its meaning as used in the passage. In the right column, write a sentence that illustrates a different meaning of the word.

Word/Meaning in the Passage	Sentence That Illustrates a Different Meaning

B. Challenge!

Write two sentences that demonstrate different meanings for one of the following words: *toll, dominion, round, course, general*.

____

____

NAME ____ DATE __________

ACTIVE READING: PREVIEW AND ACTIVATE PRIOR KNOWLEDGE

Introduction

When you read, you very often use the knowledge you already have about a subject to understand and predict the outcome of a selection. This is called **activating prior knowledge.**

Reading Tip
Activate prior knowledge by asking yourself the following questions:
1. Does the title of the piece give any clues to its contents?
2. What is the subject of the writing?
3. What do I already know about the subject?
4. Have I read about the subject before? What did I learn?

Read the following passage from "We'll Never Conquer Space" by Arthur C. Clarke. Refer to the reading tip, and answer the questions posed there. For example, the title, the author's name, and the first sentence reveal that the passage relates to space exploration. Do you already know or have you reading anything about the space program, astronauts, or space travel? Compare your own answers with the answers that follow the passage.

> Man will never conquer space. Such a statement may sound ludicrous, now that our rockets are already 100 million miles beyond the moon and the first human travelers are preparing to leave the atmosphere. Yet it expresses a truth which our forefathers knew, one we have forgotten— and our descendants must learn again, in heartbreak and loneliness.
>
> Our age is in many ways unique, full of events and phenomena which never occurred before and can never happen again. They distort our thinking, making us believe that what is true now will be true forever, though perhaps on a larger scale. Because we have annihilated distance on this planet, we imagine that we can do it once again. The facts are far otherwise....

Sample: Activate Prior Knowledge

1. What I already know: Human beings have landed on the moon.
2. What I've read about this subject before: The space program repaired the Hubble telescope and is exploring how to establish and maintain a space station.

Practice

Below is another passage from "We'll Never Conquer Space." Answer the questions that follow the passage.

The marvelous telephone and television network that will soon enmesh the whole world, making all men neighbors, cannot be extended into space. It will never be possible to converse with anyone on another planet.

Do not misunderstand this statement. Even with today's radio equipment, the problem of sending speech to the other planets is almost trivial. But the messages will take minutes—sometimes hours—on their journey, because radio and light waves travel at the same limited speed of 186,000 miles a second.

Twenty years from now you will be able to listen to a friend on Mars, but the words you hear will have left his mouth at least three minutes earlier, and your reply will take a corresponding time to reach him. In such circumstances, an exchange of verbal messages is possible—but not a conversation.

1. Before you read the second passage, how did you predict that Clarke would support his argument that "we'll never conquer space"?

   ____

   ____

2. Did the second passage cause you to activate any prior knowledge about science? If so, what?

   ____

   ____

3. In the second passage, what distinction does Clarke draw between "an exchange of verbal messages" and "a conversation"? How does this distinction support his claim that "we'll never conquer space"?

   ____

   ____

   ____

   ____

ACTIVE READING: SET A PURPOSE

Introduction

Different types of writing present different reasons for reading. For example, we usually read textbooks to gather information, and we read stories for pleasure. The first sentence or paragraph of a selection will often indicate the kind of writing that follows. For example, when you read the passage below, you can make a reliable inference about the kind of material that will follow.

Asking Questions to Set a Purpose

Setting a purpose for reading involves identifying specific questions that you will answer during reading. By asking yourself questions before you begin, you direct your attention to the key ideas in the passage. You can get an idea of what the selection is about by looking at the title, illustrations, and subheadings. You may also want to read the first sentence or paragraph for further information.

Setting a Purpose: Three Steps

1. Study the title and illustrations of a selection.
2. Read the first sentence or paragraph.
3. Look for clues in the text. Is the writing informative? Persuasive? Entertaining?

Model

Read the following passage from the beginning of "Wartime Speech" by Winston Churchill. Think of questions you could use to set a purpose for reading the entire selection. Then compare your ideas with the ones below.

> I speak to you for the first time as Prime Minister in a solemn hour for the life of our country, of our Empire, of our Allies, and, above all, of the cause for Freedom. A tremendous battle is raging in France and Flanders....

Questions

What kind of writing is this?
- A speech

Purpose for Reading

Why would someone choose to read this passage?
- For enjoyment
- To learn more about Churchill as a wartime leader
- To find out about a major turning point in history

NAME _______________________________   **DATE** _____________

Practice

Below is a passage from *A History of the English Church and People* by Bede.
Read the passage and answer the questions that follow.

> Britain, formerly known as Albion, is an island in the ocean, facing
> between north and west, and lying at a considerable distance from the
> coasts of Germany, Gaul, and Spain, which together form the greater
> part of Europe. It extends 800 miles northwards, and is 200 in breadth,
> except where a number of promontories stretch farther, the coastline
> round which extends to 3,675 miles....Britain is rich in grain and timber;
> it has good pasturage for cattle and draft animals, and vines are culti-
> vated in various localities. There are many land and sea birds of various
> species, and it is well known for its plentiful springs and rivers abounding
> in fish.

1. What kind of a selection do you think this is?

   ____

   ____

2. What might be your purpose for reading this selection? Why?

   ____

   ____

Below is a list of several different types of selections. What might be your
purpose for reading each of these types of selections? Explain.

3. a comic drama

   ____

   ____

4. an editorial

   ____

   ____

5. a chapter on another country in a social studies textbook

   ____

   ____

6. a magazine article about a sports star

   ____

   ____

7. an instruction manual

   ____

   ____

Comprehension STRATEGY

ACTIVE READING: QUESTION AND CLARIFY

Introduction

Question: Asking yourself questions while you read can help improve your reading comprehension. The first step is to identify what is confusing to you.

Clarify: You will probably find the answer to your question by stopping to think; looking back over material you have already read; consulting any footnotes or glosses that are provided with the passage; or continuing to read on, keeping your question in mind. Sometimes, when the meaning of a word is the source of your confusion, looking up the word in a dictionary will help clarify the sentence or passage.

Question	Clarify
Establish specific point of confusion	Stop and think
Construct question	Reread confusing part Consult footnotes or dictionary Read ahead to see if new information clarifies confusing part

Model

Read the passage below from *The Rape of the Lock* by Alexander Pope. Note the reader's questions and answers in italics.

Close by those meads, forever crowned with flowers,
Where Thames with pride surveys his rising towers,

What is "meads"? I guess it's short for "meadows," because Pope mentions "flowers" in the same line. The Thames is the river in London.

There stands a structure of majestic frame,[1]
Which from the neighboring Hampton takes its name.

What is this building? Oh, I see—it's explained in the footnote.

Here Britain's statesmen oft the fall foredoom
Of foreign tyrants, and of nymphs at home;
Here thou, great Anna![2] whom three realms obey,
Dost sometimes counsel take—and sometimes tea.

This line confused me, but I see now that the verb "take" has two objects: "counsel" and "tea."

---

1. **structure…frame:** Hampton court, a royal palace near London.
2. **Anna:** Queen Anne, who ruled England, Ireland, and Scotland from 1702 through 1714.

Practice

Below is another passage from *The Rape of the Lock* by Alexander Pope. As you read the passage, ask yourself questions about what is happening.

> Hither the heroes and the nymphs resort,
> To taste awhile the pleasures of a court;
> In various talk th'instructive hours they passed,
> Who gave the ball, or paid the visit last;
> One speaks the glory of the British Queen,
> And one describes a charming Indian screen;
> A third interprets motions, looks, and eyes;
> At every word a reputation dies.

A. What were some questions you asked yourself while reading this passage? Write your questions and answers in the space below. Tell you arrived at your answers.

____

____

____

____

____

____

B. Challenge!
Select another passage from *The Rape of the Lock* or from another piece of literature. As you read, write down questions that come to mind. Then try to answer those questions, and explain how you arrived at your answers.

____

____

____

____

____

____

ACTIVE READING: CONNECT

Introduction

Understanding what you read requires that you connect to the text in some way. Often you will be reminded of something else you once read, or you may even have had a similar personal experience to the one described.

Everyone connects to a text in a unique and individual way. The way that you think about and connect to characters, events, comments, or descriptions in the text may be very different from the manner in which a friend or classmate relates to these elements. Some of the connections that you will likely have in common with friends or classmates, however, involve the links you can make by relating ideas within the text.

Here is a helpful list of the various ways that you can actively connect to a text as you read:

- Connect what is said with your own ideas and feelings.
- Connect what is described with experiences from your own life.
- Connect what is said with other texts such as stories or articles that you have read.
- Connect the ideas, characters, events, or descriptions within the text to each other.

Model

The passage below is from "The Fiddle" by Alan Sillitoe. As you read the passage, make your own connections. Some typical connections you might make are listed below.

> "I'd do anything," he repeated to his mother over his tea in the single room downstairs.
>
> "But what, though?" she asked. "What can you do, Jeff?"
>
> "Well, how do I know?" he almost snapped at her. "But I'll do summat,[1] you can be sure of that."
>
> He didn't do anything till the weather got better and life turned a bit sweeter. Maybe this improvement finally got him going, because it's hard to help yourself towards better things when you're too far down in the dumps.

---

1. summat: Something.

If asked, a person might mention these types of connections:

- personal memories and thoughts of anxiety or frustration
- the familiar setting of a conversation with a parent
- the experience of feeling depressed or trying to make a tough decision
- the way weather can occasionally affect a person's moods

NAME ____ DATE ___________

Practice

Below is another passage from "The Fiddle." As you read the selection, think about how you connect to it.

> "It'll be enough," he said roughly.
>
> "Enough for what, Jeff?"
>
> He didn't say, but the fact that he had sold his fiddle for four quid rattled up and down the line of cottages till everybody knew of it. Others swore he'd got ten pounds for it, because something that made such music must be worth more than a paltry four, and in any case Jeff would never say how much he'd really got for it, for fear that someone would go in and rob him.
>
> They wondered why he'd done it, but had to wait for the answer, as one usually does....
>
> All he'd done was make up his mind, and he'd done that lying on his side at the pit face while ripping coal out with his pick and shovel. Decisions made like that can't be undone, he knew. He'd brooded on it all winter, till the fact of having settled it seemed to have altered the permanent expression of his face, and given it a new look which caused people to wonder whether he would ever be able to play the fiddle again anyway—at least with his old spirit and dash.

Now, make a list of the ideas, comments, or descriptions from the passage that you connect to. Write down even the simplest connections that occur to you. Also, consider how aspects of the passage relate to each other. Then, briefly describe the connections in the space provided.

Phrase From the Passage	Connection
1.	
2.	
3.	
4.	
5.	
6.	
7.	

ACTIVE READING: KWL

Introduction

By determining how you will read and by thinking about what you read, you can become an active reader. Whether you read a story or a work of nonfiction, you may want to use a strategy known as **KWL** to get the most out of a selection. The letters *KWL* stand for *Know, Want,* and *Learn.* To use the KWL strategy, follow these steps:

- Brainstorm about what you *know* concerning the subject before you read. Think about main concepts, facts, and details.
- Before you read, list what you *want* to learn as a result of reading the selection. Write down questions that you have about this subject. You may want to find answers to such questions as *who, what, where, when, why,* and *how.*
- After you finish reading, evaluate what you have *learned* about this subject. List new information you gained as a result of your reading.

Model

You may want to use a chart like the one shown below to help you organize what you already know about a subject, what you want to learn, and what you learn as a result of your reading.

K (What I Know)	W (What I Want to Learn)	L (What I Learned)

Reading Tips

- Jot down these questions in order to help you remember the steps involved in using the KWL strategy: What do I Know? What do I Want to learn? What did I Learn?
- Before you read a selection, list what you already know about a subject. Then list what you want to find out about the subject in the form of questions. As you read, look for the answers to these questions.
- If your questions about a subject were not answered in the reading, use different sources of information—encyclopedias, people in the community, textbooks—to help you answer them.

Practice

Below is a passage from Daniel Defoe's *A Journal of the Plague Year,* about the great plague that devastated London in the year 1665. Before you read, fill in the first two columns of the KWL chart. First, write what you know about the plague. Next, write what you want to learn about this historical event. Then, read the passage. After you finish, write what you learned.

> The face of London was now indeed strangely altered, I mean the whole mass of cities, buildings, liberties, suburbs, Westminster, Southwark, and altogether; for as to the particular part called the city, or within the walls, that was not yet much infected. But in the whole the face of things, I say, was much altered; sorrow and sadness sat upon every face; and though some parts were not yet overwhelmed, yet all looked deeply concerned; and as we saw it apparently coming on, so everyone looked on himself and his family as in the utmost danger. Were it possible to represent those times exactly to those that did not see them, and give the reader due ideas of the horror that everywhere presented itself, it must make just impressions upon their minds and fill them with surprise. London might well be said to be all in tears; the mourners did not go about the streets indeed, for nobody put on black or made a formal dress of mourning for their nearest friends; but the voice of mourning was truly heard in the streets. The shrieks of women and children at the windows and doors of their houses, where their dearest relations were perhaps dying, or just dead, were so frequent to be heard as we passed the streets, that it was enough to pierce the stoutest heart in the world to hear them. Tears and lamentations were seen almost in every house, especially in the first part of the visitation; for toward the latter end men's hearts were hardened, and death was so always before their eyes, that they did not so much concern themselves for the loss of their friends, expecting that themselves should be summoned the next hour....

The Great Plague in London

K (What I Know)	W (What I Want to Learn)	L (What I Learned)

IDENTIFY MAIN IDEA AND SUPPORTING DETAILS

Introduction

Effective readers look for the most important point a writer is trying to make. This helps them to create meaning, or make sense of the text. The central idea in a passage is its **main idea.** The main idea can appear at the beginning, middle, or end of a passage, and it may be stated or implied.

- A **stated main idea** is one in which the central idea of the passage is clearly stated in one sentence in the selection.
- An **implied main idea** is not stated in any single sentence. Instead, it is revealed indirectly through the connections among the details in the passage.

Writers support main ideas with **supporting details**. When you are reading, it is important to recognize these words, phrases, or sentences that tell something about the main idea. These details can be facts, statistics, dates, names or opinions.

Model

Look for the main idea and supporting details in this passage from an essay by Samuel Johnson. Compare your answers with the ones below:

> As Pride sometimes is hid under humility, Idleness is often covered by turbulence and hurry…. Some are always in a state of preparation, occupied in previous measures, forming plans, accumulating materials, and providing for the main affair. These are certainly under the secret power of Idleness. Nothing is to be expected from the workman whose tools are forever to be sought. I was once told by a great master, that no man ever excelled in painting, who was eminently curious about pencils and colors.

Main Idea

- Idleness is often covered by turbulence and hurry.

This sentence clearly states the central idea of the paragraph: People often conceal their own idleness by pretending to be busy.

Supporting Details

- Some people are always preparing for a job and never actually doing it.
- Nothing is to be expected from a workman who can never find his tools.
- An artist who fusses about the tools of his trade will never be a good painter.

These details are examples that support and illustrate the main idea. The writer is not specifically interested in telling the reader a story about workmen or painters. He mentions these details to give weight to his main idea about idleness.

Practice

Part I

Below is a passage from "The Preface to *A Dictionary of the English Language*" by Samuel Johnson. Read the passage, and answer the questions that follow.

> When I took the first survey of my understanding, I found our speech copious without order and energetic without rule; wherever I turned my view, there was perplexity to be disentangled and confusion to be regulated; choice was to be made out of boundless variety, without any established principle of selection; adulterations were to be detected, without a settled test of purity; and modes of expression to be rejected or received, without the suffrages of any writers of classical reputation or acknowledged authority.

1. What statement best expresses the main idea of this passage? Explain your answer.

   ____

   ____

   ____

   ____

2. Is the main idea implied or stated? _______________________________

3. Identify three supporting details in the passage. Write the details in the spaces provided. Explain how each detail supports the main idea.

   a. ____

   ____

   b. ____

   ____

   c. ____

   ____

Practice

Part II

Below is a passage from the epic *Paradise Lost* by John Milton. The
passage is part of a speech by Satan as he enters Hell for the first time.
Read the passage, and then answer the questions that follow.

> Hail horrors! Hail
> Infernal world! and thou, profoundest Hell
> Receive thy new possessor, one who brings
> A mind not to be changed by place or time.
> The mind is its own place, and in itself
> Can make a Heaven of Hell, a Hell of Heaven.
> What matter where, if I be still the same,
> And what I should be, all but less than he
> Whom thunder hath made greater? Here at least
> We shall be free; the Almighty hath not built
> Here for his envy, will not drive us hence;
> Here we may reign secure, and in my choice
> To reign is worth ambition though in Hell:
> Better to reign in Hell than serve in Heaven.

1. What statement best expresses the main idea of this passage? Explain
   your answer.

   ____

   ____

   ____

   ____

2. Is the main idea implied or stated? _______________________________

3. Identify three supporting details in this passage. Write the details in
   the spaces provided. Explain how each detail supports the main idea.

   a. ____

   ____

   b. ____

   ____

   c. ____

   ____

     Identify Main Ideas and Supporting Details   **33**

Part III

Below is a passage from "The Demon Lover," a short story by Elizabeth
Bowen. Read the passage, and then answer the questions that follow.

> Toward the end of her day in London Mrs. Drover went round to her shut-
> up house to look for several things she wanted to take away. Some belonged
> to herself, some to her family, who were by now used to their country life.
> It was late August; it had been a steamy, showery day; at the moment the
> trees down the pavement glittered in an escape of humid yellow afternoon
> sun. Against the next patch of clouds, already piling up ink-dark, broken
> chimneys and parapets stood out. In her once familiar street, as in any
> unused channel, an unfamiliar queerness had silted up; a cat wove itself
> in and out of railings, but no human eye watched Mrs. Drover's return.
> Shifting some parcels under her arm, she slowly forced round her latchkey
> in an unwilling lock, then gave the door, which had warped, a push with
> her knee. Dead air came out to meet her as she went in.

1. What statement best expresses the main idea of this passage? Explain
   your answer.

   ____

   ____

   ____

   ____

2. Is the main idea implied or stated? _______________________________

3. Identify three supporting details in this passage. Write the details in
   the spaces provided. Explain how each detail supports the main idea.

   a. ____

   ____

   b. ____

   ____

   c. ____

   ____

MAKE INFERENCES

Introduction

An **inference** is a reasonable guess or logical conclusion. Making inferences allows you to figure out things that aren't explicitly stated. Effective readers make inferences all the time as they read. They think carefully about the information they are given and combine it with their own knowledge about people and life in general.

From this combination, they are able to make inferences or logical conclusions that help them to understand the text. Although you may often make inferences unconsciously, at other times you may need to read carefully between the lines and think about what is said.

Helpful Hint

Keep this equation in mind to understand how you make inferences:

Textual Clues + What You Know = Inference

Model

Read the passage below from "The Rocking-Horse Winner" by D. H. Lawrence. Then see if the inferences you made match the ones listed below.

> When there were no visitors, Paul now took his meals with his parents, as he was beyond the nursery control. His mother went into town nearly every day. She had discovered that she had an odd knack of sketching furs and dress materials, so she worked secretly in the studio of a friend who was the chief "artist" for the leading drapers. She drew the figures of ladies in furs and ladies in silk and sequins for the newspaper advertisements. This young woman artist earned several thousand pounds a year, but Paul's mother only made several hundreds, and she was again dissatisfied. She so wanted to be first in something, and she did not succeed, even in making sketches for drapery advertisements.

Inference: Paul's mother has artistic talent.
Support for this inference: *The passage says that she had an odd knack of sketching furs and dress materials.*

Inference: Paul's mother is too proud to admit that she needs to work to earn money.
Support for this inference: *The passage says that she works secretly.*

Inference: Paul's mother is ambitious.
Support for this inference: *The passage says that she is dissatisfied with her earnings and wants to be first in something.*

Practice

Below is another passage from D. H. Lawrence's story "The Rocking-Horse Winner." Read the passage, and practice making inferences by using the chart below.

> "Surely you're too big for a rocking horse!" his mother had remonstrated.
>
> "Well, you see, mother, till I can have a *real* horse, I like to have some sort of animal about," had been his quaint answer.
>
> "Do you feel he keeps you company?" she laughed.
>
> "Oh, yes! He's very good, he always keeps me company, when I'm there," said Paul.
>
> So the horse, rather shabby, stood in an arrested prance in the boy's bedroom.
>
> The Derby was drawing near, and the boy grew more and more tense. He hardly heard what was spoken to him, he was very frail, and his eyes were really uncanny. His mother had sudden strange seizures of uneasiness about him. Sometimes, for half an hour, she would feel a sudden anxiety about him that was almost anguish. She wanted to rush to him at once, and know he was safe.

Make five different inferences about this passage by using this chart.

Textual Clues	+	What You Know	=	Inference
1. "Surely you're too big for a rocking horse!" his mother had remonstrated.				
2. "Do you feel he keeps you company?" she laughed.				
3. "…I like to have some sort of animal about," had been his quaint answer.				
4. The Derby was drawing near, and the boy was growing more and more tense.				
5. …he was very frail, and his eyes were really uncanny.				
6. His mother had sudden strange seizures of uneasiness about him.				

COMPARE AND CONTRAST

Introduction

As you read, look for the writer's use of comparisons and contrasts. A writer uses **comparison** to show how things are similar and **contrast** to show how things are different. Recognizing comparisons and contrasts will help you identify relationships between people, places, and things you encounter in your reading.

Reading Tip

Look for clue words that may help you recognize a comparison or a contrast. Clue words and phrases that may signal a comparison are *like, similar to, resembles, just as,* and *the same.* Clue words and phrases that may signal a contrast are *but, yet, unlike, different from, however,* and *nevertheless.*

Model

In the passage below, from Virginia Woolf's short story "The Duchess and the Jeweller," look for ways in which the writer uses comparisons and contrast to describe the Duchess and to indicate her relationship with Oliver Bacon, the jeweler.

> As a parasol with many flounces, as a peacock with many feathers, shuts its flounces, folds its feathers, so she subsided and shut herself as she sank down in the leather armchair.
>
> "Good morning, Mr. Bacon," said the Duchess. And she held out her hand which came through the slit of her white glove. And Oliver bent low as he shook it. And as their hands touched the link was forged between them once more. They were friends, yet enemies; he was master, she was mistress; each cheated the other, each needed the other, each feared the other, each felt this and knew this every time they touched hands….

Comparison

- The Duchess is like a parasol or a peacock.
- The Duchess and the jeweler are alike in their needs, their fears, and their deceptions.

Contrast

- The Duchess and the jeweler are friends but also enemies.

Clue Words

as…so (signals a comparison)
yet (signals a contrast)

                    Compare and Contrast **37**

NAME ____   **DATE** _____________

Practice

Below is a passage from *Utopia* by Sir Thomas More. Read the passage, and answer the questions that follow.

> When a ruler enjoys wealth and pleasure while all about him are grieving and groaning, he acts as a jailor rather than as a king. He is a poor physician who cannot cure a disease except by throwing his patient into another. A king who can only rule his people by taking from them the pleasures of life shows that he does not know how to govern free men. He ought to shake off either his sloth or his pride, for the people's hatred and scorn arise from these faults in him. Let him live on his own income without wronging others, and limit his expenses to his revenue. Let him curb crime, and by his wise conduct prevent it rather than allow it to increase, only to punish it subsequently. Let him not rashly revive laws already abrogated by disuse, especially if they have been long forgotten and never wanted. And let him never seize any property on the ground that it is forfeited as a fine, when a judge would regard a subject as wicked and fraudulent for claiming it.

1. In the first sentence, what comparison does More draw between a selfish, pleasure-loving ruler and a jailor?

   ____

   ____

2. Explain the implied comparison involving a physician that More uses in the second sentence.

   ____

   ____

3. What are three ways in which More contrasts a good ruler with a bad ruler in this passage?

   a. ____

   ____

   b. ____

   ____

   c. ____

   ____

NAME ____   **DATE** _____________

IDENTIFY STEPS IN A PROCESS
OR FOLLOW A SEQUENCE OF EVENTS

Introduction

To understand what you read, you need to understand how events are connected. Events in our lives occur in a time order or **sequence of events.** This happens in literary selections as well. When you are reading, notice how writers provide clue words or phrases such as *first, second, finally, when, then, next, later, to begin with, eventually, in the end,* and so forth to indicate the passage of time.

Model

In this passage from George Orwell's essay "Shooting an Elephant," look for the sequence of events. Notice that the author uses clue phrases such as *in the end, later, before, by the afternoon,* and *afterwards* to indicate the passage of time or the sequence of events.

> In the end I could not stand it any longer and went away. I heard later that it took him half an hour to die. Burmans were bringing dahs and baskets even before I left, and I was told they had stripped his body almost to the bones by the afternoon.
>
> Afterwards, of course, there were endless discussions about the shooting of the elephant....

NAME ______________________________   DATE ______________

Practice

Read this passage from "No Witchcraft for Sale" by Doris Lessing. Then answer the questions that follow.

> Eventually, when the meal was over, the Farquars called Gideon into their living room and explained to him that this baas, here, was a Big Doctor from the Big City, and he had come all that way to see Gideon. At this Gideon seemed afraid; he did not understand; and Mrs. Farquar explained quickly that it was because of the wonderful thing he had done with Teddy's eyes that the Big Baas had come.
>
> Gideon looked from Mrs. Farquar to Mr. Farquar, and then at the little boy, who was showing great importance because of the occasion. At last he said grudgingly: "The Big Bass want to know what medicine I used?" He spoke incredulously, as if he could not believe his old friends could so betray him. Mr. Farquar began explaining how a useful medicine could be made out of the root, and how it could be put on sale, and how thousands of people, black and white, up and down the continent of Africa, could be saved by the medicine when that spitting snake filled their eyes with poison.

1. List all the clue words and phrases that the author uses to indicate the passage of time and the sequence of events.

   ____

   ____

2. Without looking at the above passage, put the events listed below in the correct sequence by writing 1, 2, 3, and so forth in the blanks provided.
   a. _____ Gideon looked at the family and asked a question grudgingly.
   b. _____ Gideon used medicine to cure young Teddy's eyes.
   c. _____ The Farquars and their visitor finished lunch.
   d. _____ Mr. Farquar explained how thousands of people could be cured.
   e. _____ The Farquars called Gideon into their living room.

Challenge!

3. Write a few sentences about a typical day in your life. Use time order to indicate the sequence of events in your writing. Include clue words and phrases such as *then, finally, later that day,* and so forth to indicate the passage of time.

   ____

   ____

   ____

   ____

NAME _______________________________________   DATE _______________

RECOGNIZE SPATIAL RELATIONSHIPS

Introduction

Spatial order is the organization of details according to their arrangement in space as seen by an observer. For example, you might read a descriptive paragraph in which a large building is described from top to bottom or a stage set is described from side to side. When you read, it is important to recognize **spatial relationships**, so that you can visualize what is being described.

When you read a descriptive passage, you may encounter any of these spatial relationships:

top to bottom	left to right	front to back
bottom to top	right to left	inside to outside
side to side	back to front	near to far

Transitional words and phrases, such as those listed below, often signal spatial relationships:

above	between	next to
across	down	over
behind	in the middle of	under
below	inside	up

Model

This passage is from "The Lagoon" by Joseph Conrad. Look for spatial relationships in the passage. Notice the underlined transitional words and phrases that signal these relationships.

> The men poled in the shoaling water. The creek broadened, opening out into a wide sweep of a stagnant lagoon. The forests receded from the marshy bank, leaving a level strip of bright green, reedy grass to frame the reflected blueness of the sky. A fleecy pink cloud drifted high above, trailing the delicate coloring of its image under the floating leaves and the silvery blossoms of the lotus. A little house, perched on high piles, appeared black in the distance. Near it, two tall nibong palms, that seemed to have come out of the forests in the background, leaned slightly over the ragged roof, with a suggestion of sad tenderness and care in the droop of their leafy and soaring heads.

NAME ___________________________________ **DATE** ___________

Practice

A. Below is a passage from "The Lady of Shalott" by Alfred, Lord Tennyson. Read the passage, and circle five transitional words and phrases that signal spatial relationships.

> On either side the river lie
> Long fields of barley and of rye,
> That clothe the wold[1] and meet the sky;
> And through the field the road runs by
> 5   To many-towered Camelot,
> And up and down the people go,
> Gazing where the lilies blow[2]
> Round an island there below,
>   The island of Shalott.
>
> 10   Willows whiten, aspens quiver,
> Little breezes dusk and shiver
> Through the wave that runs forever
> By the island in the river
>   Flowing down to Camelot.
> 15   Four gray walls, and four gray towers,
> Overlook a space of flowers,
> And the silent isle imbowers
>   The Lady of Shalott.

1. **wold:** Rolling plains.
2. **blow:** Bloom.

B. Challenge!

On a separate piece of paper, write a brief description of your classroom, using transitional words and phrases to show spatial relationships.

RECOGNIZE CAUSE AND EFFECT

Introduction

A **cause** is an event, action, or feeling that produces a result. An **effect** is the result that is produced by a cause. Recognizing cause-and-effect relationships can help the reader follow a literary selection.

Reading Tip
Look for clue words and phrases that may help you recognize cause and effect, such as *because, so, for this reason, therefore, consequently, since, unless,* and *that is why.*

Model

Read this passage from *The Diary* by Samuel Pepys. As you read, look for causes and effects, and compare them with the ones listed below.

> *Sept. 2, 1666.* [Lord's day.] Some of our maids sitting up late last night to get things ready against our feast today, Jane called us up about three in the morning, to tell us of a great fire they saw in the city. So I rose and slipped on my night-gown, and went to her window, and thought it to be on the back side of Mark Lane at the farthest; but, being unused to such fires as followed, I though it far enough off; and so went to bed again and to sleep.

Cause
   • The maids were busy getting things ready for the feast.
This statement shows an event that produces a result.

Effect
   • They sat up late at night.
This statement shows the result produced by the event.

Cause
   • Jane wanted to inform us of the fire.
This statement shows a feeling that produces a result.

Effect
   • She called us about three in the morning.
This statement shows the result produced by a feeling.

Cause
   • Pepys thought the fire was quite far away.
This statement shows a judgment that produces a result.

Effect
   • Pepys went back to bed until seven o'clock.
This statement shows the result produced by a judgment.

NAME _________________________________ DATE _____________

Practice

Below is another passage from *The Diary* by Samuel Pepys. Read the passage, and then answer the questions that follow.

> The churches, houses, and all on fire and flaming at once; and a horrid noise the flames made, and the cracking of houses at their ruin. So home with a sad heart, and there find everybody discoursing and lamenting the fire; and poor Tom Hater come with some of his few goods saved out of his house, which is burned upon Fish Hill Street. I invite him to lie at my house, and did receive his goods, but was deceived in his lying there, the news coming every moment of the growth of the fire; so as we were forced to begin to pack up our own goods, and prepare for their removal; and did by moonshine (it being brave dry, and moonshine, and warm weather) carry much of my goods into the garden, and Mr. Hater and I did remove my money and iron chests into my cellar, as thinking that the safest place. And got my bags of gold into my office, ready to carry away, and my chief papers of accounts also there....We did put Mr. Hater, poor man, to bed a little; but he got but very little rest, so much noise being in my house, taking down of goods.

1. Write the causes for the following effects:

   a. Pepys's feeling sad when he returns home ____________________

   ____

   b. Tom Hater's arrival at Pepys's house____________________

   ____

   c. Pepys's removing his money and iron chests to the cellar________

   ____

2. a. What was the effect of the news coming every moment of the growth of the fire? ____________________

   ____

   b. According to the final sentence, what was the effect of there being so much noise that night in Pepys's house?____________________

   ____

IDENTIFY PROBLEMS AND SOLUTIONS

Introduction

Identifying the problem and solution in a text will give you a better appreciation of what you are reading. **Problems** are the challenges that people encounter. **Solutions** are the answers to those problems. As you read a text, you will often find that there is a central problem, but there may also exist many smaller problems that need to be solved. Various steps or actions may be taken to solve the problem before a final solution is reached.

Model

Read the passage below from "An Academy for Women," written by Daniel Defoe in 1697. See if your ideas about problems and solutions match those shown on the chart below.

> I have often thought it as one of the most barbarous customs in the world…that we deny the advantages of learning to women. We reproach the sex every day with folly and impertinence, while I am confident, had they the advantages of education equal to us, they would be guilty of less than ourselves….
>
> The capacities of women are supposed to be greater and their senses quicker than those of the men; and what they might be capable of being bred to is plain from some instances of female wit, which this age is not without; which upbraids us with injustice, and looks as if we denied women the advantages of education for fear they should vie with the men in their improvements.
>
> To remove this objection, and that women might have at least a needful opportunity of education in all sorts of useful learning, I propose the draft of an academy for that purpose….

Problem	Steps to Solve Problem	Solution
Women's folly	Daily criticism and reproaches	None
Unfulfilled capacities in women	Defoe writes his essay	Starting an academy for women

Practice

The passage below is from a letter written by an English noblewoman, Lady Mary Wortley Montagu, to her daughter in the 1750's. In this passage, the writer offers advice about the education of her grandchild. Read the passage, and then answer the following questions.

> I will therefore speak to you as supposing Lady Mary not only capable but desirous of learning. In that case, by all means let her be indulged in it. You will tell me, I did not make it a part of your education. Your prospect was very different from hers, as you had no defect either in mind or person to hinder, and much in your circumstances to attract, the highest offers. It seemed your business to learn how to live in the world, as it is hers to know how to be easy out of it. It is the common error of builders and parents to follow some plan they think beautiful (and perhaps is so) without considering that nothing is beautiful that is misplaced.... Thus every woman endeavors to breed her daughter a fine lady, qualifying her for a station in which she will never appear, and at the same time incapacitating her for that retirement for which she is destined....No entertainment is so cheap as reading, nor any pleasure so lasting. She will not want new fashions nor regret the loss of expensive diversions or variety of company if she can be amused with an author in her closet. To render this amusement extensive, she should be permitted to learn the languages. I have heard it lamented that boys lose so many years in mere learning of words. This is no objection to a girl, whose time is not so precious. She cannot advance herself in any profession, and has therefore more hours to spare; and as you say her memory is good she will be very agreeably employed this way.

1. What problem does Lady Montagu address in this passage?

    ____

2. What solution does she suggest to her daughter?

    ____

3. According to the passage, what are two advantages of this solution?

    a. ____

    b. ____

4. Imagine that Daniel Defoe and Lady Montagu were to hold a discussion on the topic of women's education. Do you think they would agree or disagree? Explain your answer.

    ____

    ____

NAME ________________________   DATE ___________

USE VISUAL AND GRAPHIC CLUES

Introduction

Knowing when and how to use visual and graphic sources of information is an important skill to master when you are reading. Visual and graphic sources of information may present facts and details that will help you better understand what you read. Some examples of visual and graphic sources of information that you will use are listed below:

diagrams	lists	maps
illustrations	scale drawings	schedules
tables	timelines	graphs
charts	diagrams	cartoons

A *timeline* is one kind of visual or graphic source of information that you use to find out when certain events have taken place. For example, you may want to use a timeline to find out how political, literary, and scientific events are related. The information on a timeline is arranged in rows or columns. Headings tell you what information is given in each column.

Model

Study this example of a timeline to discover the relationships between events in Britain and world events in the period 1901–1918.

British Events		World Events	
1901	Edward VII becomes king	1901	Thomas Mann publishes *Buddenbrooks*
1902	Joseph Conrad publishes *Heart of Darkness*	1903	Wright brothers build first airplane
1903	Emmeline Pankhurst founds women's suffrage group	1904	Asia: Russo-Japanese War begins
1914	Britain enters World War I	1905	Germany: Albert Einstein proposes theory of relativity
1918	Married women over thirty achieve right to vote	1917	Austria: Sigmund Freud publishes *Introduction to Psychoanalysis*
		1917	Russian Revolution

Reading Tips

- Remember that visual and graphic sources of information are pictorial representations. You may have to interpret the information that is given.
- If you encounter visual and graphic sources of information when you read, slow down. These sources may either provide information that will help you understand what you are reading or offer additional information that is not in the text.

Practice

A. Use the train schedule below to answer the questions that follow.

London to Manchester		Manchester to London	
Departures	**Arrivals**	**Departures**	**Arrivals**
*6:00 A.M.	8:40 A.M.	*5:45 A.M.	8:37 A.M.
8:30 A.M.	11:35 A.M.	8:15 A.M.	11:28 A.M.
2:10 P.M.	5:20 P.M.	1:30 P.M.	4:47 P.M.
*5:30 P.M.	8:12 P.M.	*6:05 P.M.	8:45 P.M.
*Intercity nonstop service			

1. Which nonstop train leaving London departs earliest in the
morning?

____

2. If you must be in Manchester by 11:00 A.M., which train must you
take from London?

____

3. When would you arrive in London if you left Manchester on the
1:30 P.M. train?

____

4. If you wanted to be in London by 4:30 P.M., which train must you
take from Manchester?

____

5. How long is the trip if you take the 6:05 P.M. train from Manchester
to London?

____

B. Challenge!
On a separate piece of paper, make a schedule to show when events
in your life take place during a typical day.

INTERPRET FIGURATIVE LANGUAGE

Introduction

Figurative language is language that goes beyond the literal meaning of words. Figurative language creates interesting and unusual comparisons that provide fresh ways of viewing the world by comparing unfamiliar objects and emotions to our own experience. Some common figures of speech are

- **simile:** A comparison between two seemingly dissimilar things that uses *like* or *as*. (Example: "That child has grown like a beanstalk.")
- **metaphor:** A comparison between two seemingly dissimilar things in which one thing is spoken of as if it were another. A metaphor does not use *like* or *as*. ("She's a treasure house of stories.")
- **personification:** The granting of human qualities to nonhuman things. ("The driving rain mocked my umbrella.") Hint: Personification usually involves active verbs.

Read the passage below from "The Train from Rhodesia" by Nadine Gordimer. Notice the underlined examples of figurative language.

> The stationmaster came out of his little brick station with its pointed chalet roof, feeling the creases in his serge uniform in his legs as well. (1) A stir of preparedness rippled through the squatting native vendors waiting in the dust; (2) the face of a carved wooden animal, eternally surprised, stuck out of a sack. The stationmaster's barefoot children wandered over. (3) From the gray mud huts with the untidy heads that stood within a decorated mud wall, chickens, and dogs (4) with their skin stretched like parchment over their bones, followed the piccanins down to the track. (5) The flushed and perspiring west cast a reflection, faint, without heat, upon the station....

Notice the use of personification in examples (2), (3), and (5): the face of a carved animal is given the human quality of being surprised; the mud huts are said to have heads; and the western sky is said to perspire. In example (1), the motion of the vendors is compared to a ripple. Since this comparison does not use *like* or *as*, it is a metaphor. Example (4) is a simile comparing the tightly stretched skin of the dogs to parchment.

NAME _________________________________   DATE ____________

Practice

Below is another passage from "The Train from Rhodesia" by Nadine Gordimer. Read the passage, and underline all the examples of figurative language you find. Explain what type of figurative language each item represents. Then tell what each example adds to this excerpt.

> All up and down the length of the train in the dust the artists sprang, walking bent, like performing animals, the better to exhibit the fantasy held toward the faces on the train….
>
> Give me penny, said the little ones with nothing to sell. The dogs went and sat, quite still, under the dining car, where the train breathed out the smell of meat cooking with onion.
>
> A man passed beneath the arch of reaching arms…went along under the voices and the bargaining, interrogating the wheels. Past the dogs; glancing up at the dining car where he could stare at the faces, behind glass, drinking beer, two by two, on either side of a uniform railway vase with its pale dead flower. Right to the end, to the guard's van, where the stationmaster's children had just collected their mother's two loaves of bread; to the engine itself, where the stationmaster and the driver stood talking against the steaming complaint of the resting beast.

____

____

____

____

____

____

Challenge!

Select another passage from "The Train from Rhodesia" or another literary selection that contains figurative language. Write examples of the figurative language that you find in the space below. Explain what kind of figurative language each is, and tell what it adds to the selection.

____

____

____

____

____

____

____

NAME ____ **DATE** __________

DISTINGUISH BETWEEN IMPORTANT
AND UNIMPORTANT INFORMATION

Introduction

An essential skill in critical reading is the ability to distinguish between more important and less important information. With this skill, readers can concentrate on the key points in a passage that are worth remembering. Readers can use this strategy to identify the important ideas in nonfiction: when reading a textbook, for example, or doing research for a report. It is also a useful strategy when reading fiction: for instance, to analyze story characters, setting, experiences, and events.

Here are some points to remember when you use this strategy:

Helpful Hints
- Read through the entire piece of writing before making decisions.
- Look for the *main idea* of a paragraph, passage, or text. Important information will always back up main ideas.
- Focus on the information that the *author* considers important.
- Identify details and ask yourself: "Should I remember this information?"
- Think about your decisions—why certain information is more important.

Some of the following ideas have asterisks. These are important ideas for a report on the topic "Tiger Behavior in the Wild." Can you explain why they are important and the other ideas are less important?

Today, wild tigers are found in fourteen Asian countries.
Tigers can weigh anywhere from 165 to 660 pounds.
* Tigers are largely solitary animals.
* Tigers are most active at dawn, at dusk, and during the night.
* In wildlife sanctuaries, tigers often make use of roads and trails to patrol their territories.
Only five out of eight recognized subspecies of tiger are still found in the wild today.
* Cubs remain with their mothers until the cubs are about two years old.

The asterisks indicate information that directly bears on the *behavior* of tigers.

NAME ______________________________   **DATE** ____________

Practice

Below is a passage from "Defending Nonviolent Resistance," a speech by Mohandas K. Gandhi. After you read the passage, list the information you think you should remember and the information you think is less important. Explain your decisions.

> Consequently, when the existence of the empire was threatened in 1899 by the Boer challenge, I offered my services to it, raised a volunteer ambulance corps, and served at several actions that took place for the relief of Ladysmith. Similarly in 1906, at the time of the Zulu revolt, I raised a stretcher-bearer party and served till the end of the "rebellion." On both these occasions I received medals and was even mentioned in dispatches. For my work in South Africa I was given by Lord Hardinge a Kaiser-i-hind Gold Medal. When the war broke out in 1914 between England and Germany, I raised a volunteer ambulance corps in London consisting of the then resident Indians in London, chiefly students. Its work was acknowledged by the authorities to be valuable. Lastly, in India, when a special appeal was made at the War Conference in Delhi in 1918 by Lord Chelmsford for recruits, I struggled at the cost of my health to raise a corps in Kheda, and the response was being made when the hostilities ceased and orders were received that no more recruits were wanted. In all these efforts at service I was actuated by the belief that it was possible by such services to gain a status of full equality in the empire for my countrymen.

1. Important Information:	Reason for My Decision:

2. Less Important Information:	Reason for My Decision:

DISTINGUISH BETWEEN FACT AND OPINION OR NONFACT

Introduction

Writers sometimes express an opinion as if it were a fact. Often an opinion may be supported by evidence and may appear to be factual. At times information may even be untrue, out of date, or based on a guess. It is important, therefore, that readers think about what they read and form judgments as to whether the information is fact, opinion, or nonfact.

Remember the following distinctions:
- A **statement of fact** is a piece of information that is true and may be verified by direct observation or measurement.
- A **statement of opinion** expresses a belief or judgment about something. It cannot be verified. A **valid opinion** is an opinion that is supported by evidence.
- A **nonfact** is conjecture, or a guess. It cannot be verified. It may be proved to be false.

Helpful Hints

Explicit verbal cues often signal that a statement is an opinion. These signal words include verbs such as *must* and *should.* Cues also include adjectives that state qualities such as *good, bad, best, important,* and *beautiful.*

Model

Read this passage from "A Devoted Son" by Anita Desai. Identify at least one fact, one opinion, and one nonfact. Compare your answers with the ones below.

> [He] now became known not only as the best but also the richest doctor in town.
>
> However, all this was not accomplished in the wink of an eye. Naturally not. It was the achievement of a lifetime and it took up Rakesh's whole life. At the time he set up his clinic his father had grown into an old man and retired from his post at the kerosene dealer's depot at which he had worked for forty years, and his mother died soon after, giving up the ghost with a sigh that sounded positively happy, for it was her own son who ministered to her in her last illness and who sat pressing her feet at the last moment—such a son as few women have borne.

Facts: Rakesh's father had worked at the kerosene dealer's depot for forty years before retiring; Rakesh's mother died soon afterwards; her son ministered to her in her last illness. These statements might be verified by direct observation or measurement.

Opinions: Rakesh became known as the best doctor in town. *Best* is a signal word. The mother's last sigh sounded happy. *Happy* is a signal word.

Nonfact: Rakesh was a son such as few women have borne. This is conjecture and cannot be verified. It could be proved false.

NAME ____ **DATE** ___________

Practice
Part I

Below is another passage from "A Devoted Son" by Anita Desai. Read the passage critically to distinguish between fact and opinion or nonfact. Then fill in the chart.

Old Varma nodded with melancholy triumph. "That is how he treats me—after I have brought him up, given him an education, made him a great doctor. Great doctor! This is the way great doctors treat their fathers, Bhatia," for the son's sterling personality and character now underwent a curious sea change. Outwardly all might be the same but the interpretation had altered: his masterly efficiency was nothing but cold heartlessness, his authority was only tyranny in disguise.

There was cold comfort in complaining to neighbors and, on such a miserable diet, Varma found himself slipping, weakening, and soon becoming a genuinely sick man. Powders and pills and mixtures were not only brought in when dealing with a crisis like an upset stomach but became a regular part of his diet—became his diet, complained Varma, supplanting the natural foods he craved.

Fact	Opinion	Nonfact	How I Know

NAME _______________________________________   **DATE** _______________

Part II

The passage below is from "On the Passing of the Reform Bill," a letter
written by Thomas Babington Macaulay in 1832. In this letter, Macaulay
describes a tense scene before a historic vote in the British House of
Commons. Read the passage carefully, deciding whether statements are
facts, opinions, or nonfacts. Then answer the questions that follow.

> Such a scene as the division of last Tuesday I never saw, and never expect
> to see again. If I should live fifty years the impression of it will be as fresh
> and sharp in my mind as if it had just taken place. It was like seeing
> Caesar stabbed in the Senate House…a sight to be seen only once and
> never to be forgotten. The crowd overflowed the House in every part.
> When the strangers were cleared out and the doors locked we had six
> hundred and eight members present, more by fifty five than ever were
> at a division before. The Ayes and Noes were like two vollies of cannon
> from opposite sides of a field of battle. When the opposition went out
> into the lobby,—an operation by the by which took up twenty minutes
> or more,—we spread ourselves over the benches on both sides of the
> House. For there were many of us who had not been able to find a seat
> during the evening. When the doors were shut we began to speculate on
> our numbers. Every body was desponding.

1. What facts are given about the attendance in the House of
   Commons?

   ____

   ____

2. What opinion does Macaulay express about the Ayes and Noes?

   ____

   ____

3. From the evidence of the passage, do you think Macaulay's comparison of the scene in the House of Commons to the assassination of
   Julius Caesar in ancient Rome is a valid opinion? Why or why not?

   ____

   ____

   ____

4. Is there any statement in the passage that you would classify as a
   nonfact—or an unverifiable conjecture that might be proved false?

   ____

   ____

   ____

NAME ____   **DATE** ____________

Part III

Below is an excerpt from *Gulliver's Travels* by Jonathan Swift. As you read
the passage, make a judgment about whether the information is fact,
opinion, or nonfact. List your decisions below, and explain your thinking.

> His Majesty desired I would take some other opportunity of bringing all
> the rest of his enemy's ships into his ports. And so unmeasurable is the
> ambition of princes, that he seemed to think of nothing less than reducing
> the whole empire of Blefuscu into a province and governing it by a
> viceroy…by which he would remain sole monarch of the whole world.
> But I endeavored to divert him from this design by many arguments
> drawn from the topics of policy as well as justice, and I plainly protested
> that I would never be an instrument of bringing a free and brave people
> into slavery. And when the matter was debated in council, the wisest
> part of the ministry were of my opinion.
>
> This open bold declaration of mine was so opposite to the schemes
> and politics of his Imperial Majesty that he could never forgive me; he
> mentioned it in a very artful manner at council, where I was told that
> some of the wisest appeared, at least, by their silence, to be of my opinion;
> but others, who were my secret enemies, could not forbear some expres-
> sions, which by a sidewind reflected on me.

Fact

____

____

____

____

Opinion

____

____

____

____

Nonfact

____

____

____

____

NAME ____ DATE _____________

EVALUATE AUTHOR'S PURPOSE AND POINT OF VIEW

Introduction

An **author's purpose** is the main reason that he or she has for writing a particular work of fiction or nonfiction. An author's purpose may be one of the following:

- to entertain
- to describe
- to persuade
- to inform

Many works of fiction and nonfiction have more than one purpose. When you are reading, remember that an article written to persuade readers to vote might also inform people about the locations of community polling places and about provisions for disabled voters and absentee ballots. Being able to recognize why an author has written a particular piece will help you decide on your approach to it and will also increase your understanding and appreciation of the selection.

Whether an author's purpose is to entertain, describe, persuade, or inform, the perspective that he or she takes when writing is called **point of view**. In nonfiction, the point of view is the writer's opinions or attitudes toward a subject. By reading a selection carefully and by noting details, you can draw conclusions about an author's feelings concerning the subject.

In fiction, the author chooses a point of view from which to tell the story. This vantage point or perspective may be a **first-person** or **third-person** point of view. In both cases, the narrator or teller of the story is fictional. Study the chart below to learn about the differences between these two points of view.

Who Tells the Story?

First Person	Third Person
A character in the story gives you his or her firsthand account of people and events, using the pronouns *I, me,* and *we.*	A narrator who is not one of the characters in the story tells what happens, using the pronouns *he, she, it,* and *they.*
Readers learn only what one character—the narrator—sees, thinks, and feels.	Readers may learn what one character or several characters in the story see, think, and feel.

NAME ____   **DATE** _______________

Practice

A. Complete the chart below by writing two additional examples of types of writing whose purposes are to entertain, describe, persuade, or inform. The chart has been started for you.

Entertain	Describe	Persuade	Inform
poem	character sketch	speech	news article

B. Read the passage below from "Araby," a short story by James Joyce. Then complete the sentences that follow.

One evening I went into the back drawing room in which the priest had died. It was a dark rainy evening and there was no sound in the house. Through one of the broken panes I heard the rain impinge upon the earth, the fine incessant needles of water playing in the sodden beds. Some distant lamp or lighted window gleamed below me. I was thankful that I could see so little. All my senses seemed to desire to veil themselves and, feeling that I was about to slip from them, I pressed the palms of my hands together until they trembled, murmuring: *"O love! O love!"* many times.

   At last she spoke to me. When she addressed the first words to me I was so confused that I did not know what to answer. She asked me was I going to *Araby*. I forget whether I answered yes or no. It would be a splendid bazaar, she said; she would love to go.

1. The author's purpose(s) can be identified as follows:

____

2. The point of view from which the passage is told is

____

3. This point of view reveals the thoughts and feelings of the following character or characters:

____

NAME ____   DATE ____________

EVALUATE EVIDENCE AND SOURCES OF INFORMATION

Introduction

Writers have many reasons for presenting evidence. Whatever the reason for its use, it's up to you to evaluate the reliability of pieces of evidence.

In order to evaluate the evidence, you'll have to think about its source. Is it the result of objective research? Did it come from historical documents or scholarly works? Was it drawn from interviews that include the interviewees' subjective emotions and opinions? Is it part of the author's life experience? Only when you've tried to answer these questions will you know how to evaluate the evidence presented in order to draw conclusions about what you are reading.

Keep track of the evidence you encounter by creating a chart like this:

Evidence	Probable Source	Fact or Opinion?

Model

Consider the evidence in this passage from "Condition of Ireland," an essay published in *The Illustrated London News* in 1849. Where do you think the writer got this information? From the tone of the passage, do you think it was carefully researched? Compare your answers with the ones below.

> The present condition of the Irish, we have no hesitation in saying, has been brought on by ignorant and vicious legislation. The destruction of the potato for one season, though a great calamity, would not have doomed them, fed as they were by the taxes of the state and the charity of the world, to immediate decay….When more food, more cultivation, more employment, were the requisites for maintaining the Irish in existence, the Legislature and the landlords went about introducing a species of cultivation that could only be successful by requiring fewer hands, and turning potato gardens, that nourished the maximum of human beings, into pasture grounds for bullocks, that nourished only the minimum. The Poor-Law, said to be for the relief of the people and the means of their salvation, was the instrument of their destruction.

Evidence	Probable Source	Fact or Opinion?
Legislation was faulty	economic analysis	fact?
Failure of potato crop for one year would not have doomed Irish	economic analysis; interviewees; other essays	opinion?

NAME ______________________________   **DATE** ____________

Practice

Below is another passage from "Condition of Ireland." Evaluate the evidence it presents by answering the questions.

> The land is still there, in all its natural beauty and fertility. The sparkling Shannon, teeming with fish, still flows by their doors, and might bear to them, as the Hudson and Thames bear to the people of New York and London, fleets of ships laden with wealth.…The country abounds in limestone: coal, iron, and lead have been found. It has an area of 827,994 acres, 327,237 of which are uncultivated, or occupied by woods and water. It is estimated that there are 296,000 acres of unoccupied land; and that of these 160,000 are capable of cultivation and improvement. Why are they not cultivated and improved, as the wilds of America are cultivated and improved by the brethren of the Irish? Why are these starving people not allowed and encouraged to plant their potato-gardens on the wastes?…There is about Kilrush, and in Clare, and throughout Ireland, the double melancholy spectacle of a strong man asking for work as the means for getting food; and of the fertile earth wooing his labors, in order to yield up to him its rich but latent stores; yet it lies idle and unfruitful.…[We] shall now only say that the whole of this land…is owned by a few proprietors—that many of them are absentees—that almost all are in embarrassed circumstances—and that, from ignorance, or false theory, or indolence, they prefer seeing the land covered with such misery as we have described, to either bringing the land under cultivation themselves, or allowing the people to cultivate it. Their greatest ambition, apparently, is to get rid of the people.

1. What evidence is presented to show that the economic condition of Ireland could be improved? Give two instances:

   a. ____

   b. ____

2. What do you think may have been the sources for the evidence you listed in response to question 1?

   ____

   ____

3. What additional evidence does the writer supply to show that conditions in Ireland present a "double melancholy spectacle"?

   ____

4. What evidence does the writer use to support the assertion that the greatest ambition of the proprietors seems to be to get rid of the people? Does this evidence justify the conclusion, in your view?

   ____

   ____

EVALUATE AUTHOR'S BIAS

Introduction

Two writers tackling the same subject are likely to produce quite different texts. Even if the facts are the same, the feelings, opinions, and claims expressed are not likely to correspond exactly. As you read, try to identify the writer's position or point of view. What special stake does he or she have in a particular subject? What bias might cause the author to adopt a certain point of view?

It might help to put yourself through a three-step process in order to evaluate the author's bias.

Step 1: Who is the author? What is his or her relationship to the subject?
Step 2: Which details are facts? Which are opinions?
Step 3: What bias is revealed by the author's opinions?

Opinion 1 + Opinion 2 + Opinion 3 = What bias?

Model

Read the following passage from "Words and Behavior," an essay by Aldous Huxley. Keep in mind that, when he wrote this essay in the 1930's, Huxley was concerned about the use of propaganda by governments to manipulate public feelings about warfare. As you read, try to separate facts from opinions in the passage. Finally, determine the author's bias. Compare your results with those listed below.

> Consider, for example, the case of war. War is enormously discreditable to those who order it to be waged and even to those who merely tolerate its existence. Furthermore, to developed sensibilities the facts of war are revolting and horrifying. To falsify these facts, and by doing so to make war seem less evil than it really is, and our own responsibility in tolerating war less heavy, is doubly to our advantage. By suppressing and distorting the truth, we protect our sensibilities and preserve our self-esteem. Now, language is, among other things, a device which men use for suppressing and distorting the truth. Finding the reality of war too unpleasant to contemplate, we create a verbal alternative to that reality, parallel with it, but in quality quite different from it.

Step 1: Who is writing about the subject of language and war? An author.
Step 2: The facts? (a) Language can be used to distort the truth.
(b) People can sometimes protect themselves by suppressing the truth. (c) War is an unpleasant reality.
The opinions? (a) The facts of war are revolting. (b) We create a verbal alternative to war that conceals war's reality.
Step 3: Bias of the author? He is a writer who analyzes language more carefully than most other people would.

                    Evaluate Author's Bias **61**

Practice

Below is another passage from "Words and Behavior" by Aldous Huxley.
Read the passage, and then answer the questions below.

> What is absurd and monstrous about war is that men who have no personal
> quarrel should be trained to murder one another in cold blood. By per-
> sonifying opposing armies or countries, we are able to think of war as a
> conflict between individuals. The same result is obtained by writing about
> war as though it were carried on exclusively by the generals in command
> and not by the private soldiers in their armies….The implication in both
> cases is that war is indistinguishable from a bout of fisticuffs in a bar room.
> Whereas in reality it is profoundly different. A scrap between two indi-
> viduals is forgivable; mass murder, deliberately organized, is a monstrous
> iniquity….When we talk about war, we use a language which conceals or
> embellishes its reality. Ignoring the facts, so far as we possibly can, we
> imply that battles are not fought by soldiers, but by things, principles,
> allegories, personified collectivities, or (at the most human) by opposing
> commanders, pitched against one another in single combat.

1. Name at least two opinions expressed in this selection.

   ____

   ____

2. Suppose this passage were written by someone who believed that war,
   under certain circumstances, was justifiable or even glorious. Choose
   a sentence from the passage, and rewrite it from that person's particular bias.

   ____

   ____

   ____

3. Does this passage express your attitude toward war? How is your
   attitude different from or similar to that of Aldous Huxley?

   ____

   ____

   ____

4. How might your own attitude be linked to a bias you hold, either
   consciously or unconsciously? What experiences may have influ-
   enced you to adopt the point of view you hold about war?

   ____

   ____

DRAW CONCLUSIONS

Introduction

Not all writing states conclusions. It's up to you to gather evidence and **draw conclusions** from it. In persuasive essays, your conclusions may be related to whether or not you agree with the author. In stories, novels, or dramas, the evidence might lead to a conclusion about what a character is like. The important thing is that conclusions should be based on facts and ideas presented.

As you read, jot down some of the conclusions you draw. Then list the facts that led you to them. You might use this form to record your conclusions and supporting facts.

Conclusion: ____

Facts: ____

Model

Read this passage from the play *A Man for All Seasons* by Robert Bolt. What are your conclusions about what is happening? What facts support these conclusions? Compare your responses with those below.

> **HENRY.** I will judge of your abilities, Thomas….Did you know that Wolsey named you for Chancellor?
>
> **MORE.** Wolsey!
>
> **HENRY.** Aye, before he died. Wolsey named you and Wolsey was no fool.
>
> **MORE.** He was a statesman of incomparable ability, Your Grace.
>
> **HENRY.** Was he? Was he so? [*He rises*] Then why did he fail me? Be seated— it was villainy then. Yes, villainy. I was right to break him; he was all pride, Thomas; a proud man; pride right through. And he failed me! [*More opens his mouth*] He failed me in the one thing that mattered! The one thing that matters, Thomas, then or now….[*Offhand*] Touching this matter of my divorce, Thomas; have you thought about it since we last talked?
>
> **MORE.** Of little else.
>
> **HENRY.** Then you see your way clear to me?
>
> **MORE.** That you should put away Queen Catherine, Sire? Oh alas [*He thumps the chair in distress*] as I think of it I see so clearly that I can not come with Your Grace that my endeavor is not to think of it at all.
>
> **HENRY.** Then you have not thought enough!

Conclusion: Henry wants Thomas More to support his divorce.
Facts: Henry criticizes Wolsey's pride; he brings up the subject of the divorce; he tells More that More has not thought enough about the subject.
Conclusion: More is respectful but firm in his opinions.
Facts: He speaks to the king respectfully; he tells Henry directly that he cannot support the divorce.

Practice

Read the passage below, which is also from Robert Bolt's *A Man for All Seasons*. Cross out the conclusions that are incorrect. List the supporting facts under the correct conclusions.

> **HENRY.** [*Reprovingly*] Thomas, Thomas, does a man need a Pope to tell him when he's sinned? It was a sin, Thomas; I admit it; I repent. And God has punished me; I have no son….Son after son she's borne me, Thomas, all dead at birth, or dead within the month; I never saw the hand of God so clear in anything….I have a daughter, she's a good child, a well-set child— But I have no son. [*He flares up*] It is my bounden *duty* to put away the Queen, and all the Popes back to St. Peter shall not come between me and my duty! How is it that you cannot see? Everyone else does.
>
> **MORE.** [*Eagerly*] Then why does Your Grace need my poor support?
>
> **HENRY.** Because you are honest. What's more to the purpose, you're known to be honest.…There are those like Norfolk who follow me because I wear the crown, and there are those like Master Cromwell who follow me because they are jackals with sharp teeth and I am their lion, and there is a mass that follows me because it follows anything that moves—and there is you.

1. **Conclusion:** Henry is determined to get rid of More.

   Facts: ____

   ____

   ____

2. **Conclusion:** Henry believes that he is not bound by the Pope's authority.

   Facts: ____

   ____

   ____

3. **Conclusion:** More's reputation for honesty is one of the main reasons that Henry wants More's support.

   Facts: ____

   ____

   ____

4. **Conclusion:** Henry dislikes his daughter.

   Facts: ____

   ____

   ____

SUMMARIZE

Introduction

Effective readers know how to **summarize**. The process starts when you separate important and unimportant information in your reading. You can then condense it into a form that can easily be remembered for retelling or rewriting. Follow these tips:

- Read the passage.
- Identify important information.
- Condense the information for easy recall.

Model

Read the passage below from *Treasure Island* by Robert Louis Stevenson. As you read, think about the main ideas of the passage. Then compare your ideas with the sample summary given below.

> Next moment we were both groping downstairs, leaving the candle by the empty chest; and the next we had opened the door and were in full retreat. We had not started a moment too soon. The fog was rapidly dispersing; already the moon shone quite clear on the next high ground on either side; and it was only in the exact bottom of the dell and round the tavern door that a thin veil still hung unbroken to conceal the first steps of our escape. Far less than half-way to the hamlet, very little beyond the bottom of the hill, we must come forth into the moonlight. Nor was this all, for the sound of several footsteps running came already to our ears, and as we looked back in their direction, a light tossing to and fro and still rapidly advancing showed that one of the newcomers carried a lantern.
>
> "My dear," said my mother suddenly, "take the money and run on. I am going to faint."
>
> This was certainly the end for both of us, I thought….We were just at the little bridge, by good fortune; and I helped her, tottering as she was, to the edge of the bank, where, sure enough, she gave a sigh and fell on my shoulder.

Summary

The narrator and his mother escape from the tavern with the money in the nick of time. However, the fog is lifting, and the narrator worries that they will be spotted in the moonlight before they reach the village. Just as they reach a small bridge, the narrator's mother faints and falls on his shoulder.

Practice

Read another passage from *Treasure Island*, and write a summary of it in the space provided below.

> My curiosity, in a sense, was stronger than my fear, for I could not remain where I was, but crept back to the bank again, whence, sheltering my head behind a bush of broom, I might command the road before our door. I was scarcely in position ere my enemies began to arrive, seven or eight of them, running hard, their feet beating out of time along the road and the man with the lantern some paces in front. Three men ran together, hand in hand; and I made out, even through the mist, that the middle man of this trio was the blind beggar. The next moment his voice showed me that I was right.
>
> "Down with the door!" he cried.
>
> "Aye, aye, sir!" answered two or three; and a rush was made…and then I could see them pause, and hear speeches passed in a lower key, as if they were surprised to find the door open. But the pause was brief, for the blind man again issued his commands. His voice sounded louder and higher, as if he were afire with eagerness and rage.

____

____

____

____

____

____

____

____

____

____

____

PARAPHRASE

Introduction

When effective readers **paraphrase**, they take an author's words and think them through using their previous knowledge and experience. Then they are ready to re-create the author's message using their own words.

Paraphrasing is a good way for you to check your understanding of a piece you've read. If you can restate information and communicate it to others, then you most likely have mastered it. Follow these tips:

- As you read, ask yourself what the author is saying.
- Think of other ways you could say the same thing.
- Look up any unfamiliar words.

Model

Read these stanzas from *The Rime of the Ancient Mariner* by Samuel Taylor Coleridge. Then study the paraphrased sample given below. Notice that while the writer of the paraphrase uses different language, the same information is presented and all essential details are included. The paraphrased version also includes new information—the identification of the poem as a ballad—which is placed in parentheses to separate it from the paraphrased work.

> It is an ancient Mariner,
> And he stoppeth one of three.
> "By thy long gray beard and glittering eye,
> Now wherefore stopp'st thou me?
>
> "The Bridegroom's doors are opened wide,
> And I am next of kin;
> The guests are met, the feast is set:
> May'st hear the merry din."

Paraphrase

The narrator of the ballad (we know it is a ballad because of the stanza form, rhythm, and rhyme scheme) recounts how an old sailor stopped one of three guests who were about to attend a wedding. Asking the old man his reason, the wedding guest said that he was the bridegroom's next of kin and that the festivities were about to begin.

NAME _______________________________   **DATE** _____________

Practice

Read another passage from *The Rime of the Ancient Mariner*, and then paraphrase the passage in the space provided below.

"One after one, by the star-dogged Moon,
Too quick for groan or sigh,
Each turned his face with a ghastly pang,
And cursed me with his eye.

"Four times fifty living men,
(And I heard nor sigh nor groan)
With heavy thump, a lifeless lump,
They dropped down one by one.

"The souls did from their bodies fly—
They fled to bliss or woe!
And every soul, it passed me by,
Like the whizz of my crossbow!"

"I fear thee, ancient Mariner!
I fear thy skinny hand!
And thou art long, and lank, and brown,
As is the ribbed sea sand.

"I fear thee and thy glittering eye,
And thy skinny hand, so brown."
"Fear not, fear not, thou Wedding Guest!
This body dropped not down."

____

____

____

____

____

____

____

____

____

____

FORM GENERALIZATIONS

Introduction

Authors often give readers specific clues which fit together like a puzzle, enabling readers to gain a broader, basic understanding of the reading material. The process of going from specific clues to broader understanding is called **forming generalizations**.

To form generalizations when you are reading, remember that you must:

- Read through the passage.
- Search for clues in the text. Look for words or actions that are repeated or are connected to each other in some way.
- Decide how these clues fit together. Is there a larger meaning when the clues are put together than when each is examined separately? Can you make an assumption about the passage that was not clear before? If so, you have formed a generalization.

Model

Read this excerpt from Alexander Pope's *An Essay on Man*. Can you form any generalizations from this passage about the speaker's view of human nature? See if your ideas agree with the examples given below.

> Know then thyself, presume not God to scan;
> The proper study of mankind is man.
> Placed on this isthmus of a middle state,
> A being darkly wise, and rudely great:
> With too much knowledge for the skeptic side,
> With too much weakness for the stoic's pride,
> He hangs between; in doubt to act or rest;
> In doubt to deem himself a god, or beast;
> In doubt his mind or body to prefer;
> Born but to die, and reasoning but to err;
> Alike in ignorance, his reason such,
> Whether he thinks too little, or too much…

Generalization

The speaker regards humans as made up of contradictory qualities, limitations, and numerous internal conflicts.

Clues From the Text

Man is said to be "a being darkly wise, and rudely great"; his knowledge is accompanied by weakness; he doubts whether to prefer his mind or his body.

NAME ___________________________ **DATE** ___________

Practice

Read this excerpt from "Elegy Written in a Country Churchyard" by
Thomas Gray. Then answer the questions that follow.

> Perhaps in this neglected spot is laid
>   Some heart once pregnant with celestial fire;
> Hands, that the rod of empire might have swayed,
>   Or waked to ecstasy the living lyre.
>
> But Knowledge to their eyes her ample page
>   Rich with the spoils of time did ne'er unroll;
> Chill Penury repressed their noble rage,
>   And froze the genial current of the soul.
>
> Full many a gem of purest ray serene
>   The dark unfathomed caves of ocean bear:
> Full many a flower is born to blush unseen,
>   And waste its sweetness on the desert air.

1. What generalization(s) can you form from this passage?

____

____

____

____

2. What clue(s) from the text did you use in forming your
   generalization(s)?

____

____

____

____

____

____

____

MAKE JUDGMENTS

Introduction

Effective readers are called upon to read critically, which includes forming their own opinions of the characters and their actions in a selection. This is called **making judgments**. When you read, gather evidence from the information given by the author, and make judgments based on that information. Remember that the judgments that you make are also based on your previous knowledge and experience. Therefore, judgments or opinions are subjective—they can vary widely from one reader to another. Keep in mind not to make a judgment before all the evidence is given.

Model

Read the following passage describing a school scene from *Hard Times* by Charles Dickens. Can you make any judgments of the characters and their actions from the information found here? See if your ideas agree with those given below.

> "Girl number twenty," said Mr. Gradgrind, squarely pointing with his square forefinger. "I don't know that girl. Who is that girl?"
>
> "Sissy Jupe, sir," explained number twenty, blushing, standing up, and curtseying.
>
> "Sissy is not a name," said Mr. Gradgrind. "Don't call yourself Sissy. Call yourself Cecilia."
>
> "It's father as calls me Sissy, sir," returned the young girl in a trembling voice, and with another curtsey.
>
> "Then he has no business to do it," said Mr. Gradgrind. "Tell him he mustn't, Cecilia Jupe. Let me see. What is your father?"
>
> "He belongs to the horse-riding, if you please, sir."
>
> Mr. Gradgrind frowned, and waved off the objectionable calling with his hand.

Judgments

- Mr. Gradgrind is overbearing, closed-minded, and insensitive. It is relatively easy to make a judgment about Mr. Gradgrind, the teacher.
- Sissy Jupe is shy and fearful.

The first point is accurate, based on the information in the passage above. Can the reader make a blanket judgment about Sissy, however, with so little information? What do you think?

NAME ____ **DATE** ____________

Practice

Read another passage from *Hard Times*, in which we learn more about
Sissy Jupe. Answer the questions that follow.

> "Suppose you were going to carpet a room. Would you use a carpet having
> representations of flowers upon it?" [said the gentleman].
>
> There being a general conviction by this time that "No, sir!" was always
> the right answer to this gentleman, the chorus of No was very strong. Only
> a few feeble stragglers said Yes; among them Sissy Jupe.
>
> "Girl number twenty," said the gentleman, smiling in the calm strength
> of knowledge.
>
> Sissy blushed, and stood up.
>
> "So you would carpet your room—or your husband's room, if you were
> a grown woman, and had a husband—with representations of flowers,
> would you," said the gentleman. "Why would you?"
>
> "If you please, sir, I am very fond of flowers," returned the girl.
>
> "And is that why you would put tables and chairs upon them, and
> have people walking over them with heavy boots?"
>
> "It wouldn't hurt them, sir. They wouldn't crush and wither if you
> please, sir. They would be the pictures of what was very pretty and pleasant,
> and I would fancy—"
>
> "Ay, ay, ay! but you mustn't fancy," cried the gentleman, quite elated
> by coming so happily to his point. "That's it! You are never to fancy."
>
> "You are not, Cecilia Jupe," Thomas Gradgrind solemnly repeated, "to
> do anything of that kind."
>
> "Fact, fact, fact!" said the gentleman. And "Fact, fact, fact!" repeated
> Thomas Gradgrind.

1. Has your judgment changed about Sissy Jupe? Why or why not?

____

____

2. What clues does Dickens offer in these passages that he is criticizing
some of the educational theories and practices of his time?

____

____

3. How valid do you think Dickens's judgments about education remain
today?

____

____

Read the following passage. Then answer the questions that follow. Write the letter of the correct answer on the line at the right.

> The gray warm evening of August had descended upon the city and a mild warm air, a memory of summer, circulated in the streets. The streets, shuttered for the repose of Sunday, swarmed with a gaily colored crowd. Like illumined pearls the lamps shone from the summits of their tall poles upon the living texture below which, changing shape and hue unceasingly, sent up into the warm gray evening air an unchanging unceasing murmur.

[James Joyce, "Two Gallants"]

1. What figure of speech does the writer use in the phrase "mild warm air, a memory of summer"?   1. ______
   A. metaphor   C. paradox
   B. simile   D. personification

2. From context clues, how would you define the meaning of the word *repose* in the second sentence?   2. ______
   A. contest   C. festival
   B. rest   D. responsibility

3. Which of the following statements is the best summary of the passage?   3. ______
   A. The crowd in the streets that evening was unusually large.
   B. The street lamps that evening could scarcely be seen.
   C. The weather that August evening was mild, and the streets swarmed with crowds.
   D. The shops were closed that evening because it was Sunday.

4. A synonym for the word *hue* in the last sentence is   4. ______
   A. shout   C. mass
   B. color   D. pursuit

Read the following passage. Then answer the questions that follow. Write the letter of the correct answer on the line at the right.

> In one way, indeed, he bade fair to ruin us, for he kept on staying week after week, and at last month after month, so that all the money had been long exhausted, and still my father never plucked up the heart to insist on having more. If ever he mentioned it, the captain blew through his nose so loudly that you might say he roared, and stared my poor father out of the room. I have seen him wringing his hands after such a rebuff, and I am sure the annoyance and the terror he lived in must have greatly hastened his early and unhappy death.

[Robert Louis Stevenson, *Treasure Island*]

5. From the passage, you can infer that   5. ______
   A. the narrator grew fond of the captain
   B. the narrator's father was intimidated by the captain
   C. the captain did not like staying at the narrator's house
   D. the captain was immensely wealthy

     Post-Test **73**

6. From which of the following is the passage most likely drawn?   6. ______
  A. a play   **C.** an editorial
  B. a speech   **D.** a novel

Read the following passage. Then answer the questions that follow. Write the letter of the correct answer on the line at the right.

> Oak, his features smudged, grimy, and undiscoverable from the smoke and heat, his smock-frock burnt into holes and dripping with water, the ash-stem of his sheep-crook charred six inches shorter, advanced with the humility stern adversity had thrust upon him up to the slight female form in the saddle. He lifted his hat with respect, and not without gallantry: stepping close to her hanging feet he said in a hesitating voice,—
>
> "Do you happen to want a shepherd, ma'am?"
>
> She lifted the wool veil tied round her face, and looked all astonishment. Gabriel and his cold-hearted darling, Bathsheba Everdene, were face to face.

[Thomas Hardy, *Far From the Madding Crowd*]

7. Which of the following contrasts is most important in the passage?   7. ______
  A. Gabriel is poor, while Bathsheba is rich
  B. Gabriel is humble and respectful, while Bathsheba is cold-hearted
  C. Gabriel is on the ground, while Bathsheba is on a horse
  D. Gabriel is practical, while Bathsheba is imaginative

8. From the description of Gabriel, you can conclude that he   8. ______
  A. does not pay enough attention to the way he dresses
  B. has just been fighting a fire
  C. does not know how to herd the sheep properly
  D. has overslept that morning

Read the following passage. Then answer the questions that follow. Write the letter of the correct answer on the line at the right.

> Saints should always be judged guilty until they are proved innocent, but the tests that have to be applied to them are not, of course, the same in all cases. In Gandhi's case the questions one feels inclined to ask are: to what extent was Gandhi moved by vanity—by the consciousness of himself as a humble, naked old man, sitting on a praying mat and shaking empires by sheer spiritual power— and to what extent did he compromise his own principles by entering politics, which of their nature are inseparable from coercion and fraud? To give a definite answer one would have to study Gandhi's acts and writings in immense detail, for his whole life was a sort of pilgrimage in which every act was significant.

[George Orwell, "Reflections on Gandhi"]

9. The writer's statement that Gandhi's whole life was "a sort of pilgrimage" is   9. ______
  A. a fact   **C.** an opinion
  B. a nonfact   **D.** a simile

POST-TEST

10. From the writer's introductory statement about saints, you can infer that he probably   10. ______
    A. does not believe in saints
    B. believes that saints do not exist in the twentieth century
    C. believes that strict tests should be applied to prove sainthood
    D. believes that Gandhi was not a saint

11. Which of the following is the best definition for the word *moved* in the second   11. ______
    sentence?
    A. removed   C. shaken
    B. motivated   D. changed

Read the following passage. Then answer the questions that follow. Write the letter of the correct answer on the line at the right.

My loving people, we have been persuaded by some, that are careful of our safety, to take heed how we commit ourselves to armed multitudes, for fear of treachery; but I assure you, I do not desire to live to distrust my faithful and loving people. Let tyrants fear; I have always so behaved myself that, under God, I have placed my chiefest strength and safeguard in the loyal hearts and good will of my subjects. And therefore I am come amongst you at this time, not as for my recreation or sport, but being resolved, in the midst and heat of the battle, to live or die amongst you all; to lay down, for my God, and for my kingdom, and for my people, my honor and my blood, even the dust.

[Queen Elizabeth I, "Speech Before Defeating the Spanish Armada"]

12. Based on the words the writer uses to describe the people, how would you   12. ______
    evaluate her opinion of them?
    A. The writer regards the people as changeable and disloyal.
    B. The writer regards the people as loving and loyal.
    C. The writer regards the people as potentially dangerous.
    D. The writer regards the people as stubborn and brave.

13. Which of the following is the best paraphrase of the second sentence in the   13. ______
    passage?
    A. I do not wish to be seen as a tyrant.
    B. Tyrants may fear the people, but I place my trust in them.
    C. Tyrants treat the people badly, so it is natural that they fear them.
    D. Some people have called me a tyrant, but I am fearless.

14. Which of the following is a synonym for *recreation* in the third sentence?   14. ______
    A. renewal   C. request
    B. amusement   D. panic

NAME ____   DATE _______________

15. Two contrasts that Queen Elizabeth makes in this passage are   15. ______
    A. between herself and her advisors and between herself and tyrants
    B. between herself and tyrants and between herself and the people
    C. between the Spanish and the English and between London and the
       countryside
    D. between the courtiers and the common people and between Spain and
       England

Read the following passage. Then answer the questions that follow. Write the letter
of the correct answer on the line at the right.

> All mankind is of one author and is one volume; when one man dies, one chapter
> is not torn out of the book, but translated into a better language; and every
> chapter must be so translated. God employs several translators; some pieces are
> translated by age, some by sickness, some by war, some by justice; but God's
> hand is in every translation, and his hand shall bind up all our scattered leaves
> again for that library where every book shall lie open to one another.

[John Donne, "Meditation 17"]

16. What aspects of the human condition does the author of this passage use figu-   16. ______
    rative language to discuss?
    A. sickness and health   C. life and death
    B. youth and marriage   D. success and failure

17. Which statement below best summarizes the passage?   17. ______
    A. Some human beings live just lives, while others are unjust.
    B. God punishes those who live unjustly.
    C. All humanity is linked together by a common destiny under God's
       providence.
    D. Death is the inevitable end of life.

18. The author's purpose in this passage is most likely   18. ______
    A. to entertain   C. to describe
    B. to inform   D. to persuade

Read the following passage. Then answer the questions that follow. Write the letter
of the correct answer on the line at the right.

> Among other stories, one was very passionate, methought of a complaint brought
> against a man in the town for taking a child from London from an infected
> house. Alderman Hooker told us it was the child of a very able citizen in Gracious
> Street, a saddler, who had buried all the rest of his children of the plague, and
> himself and wife now being shut up and in despair of escaping, did desire only
> to save the life of this little child; and so prevailed to have it received stark-naked
> into the arms of a friend, who brought it (having put it into new fresh clothes)
> to Greenwich; where upon hearing the story, we did agree that it should be
> received and kept in the town.

[Samuel Pepys, *The Diary*]

19. What did the saddler and his wife do after all the rest of their children had died   **19.** ______
of the plague?
   A. They spoke to Alderman Hooker.
   B. They took the remaining child to Greenwich.
   C. They gave the remaining child to a friend.
   D. They wrote to Pepys, requesting his aid.

20. What problem does the complaint pose for Pepys and the other officials he   **20.** ______
refers to in this passage?
   A. whether or not to allow the child to remain in the town, even though it
      comes from an infected house
   B. whether or not to overrule Alderman Hooker
   C. whether or not to allow the saddler and his wife to visit their child
   D. whether or not to visit Gracious Street personally

21. One conclusion you can draw from the passage is that   **21.** ______
   A. the plague lasted only a brief time in London
   B. the plague plunged the people of London into extraordinary hardship
      and suffering
   C. people in London carelessly risked each other's safety during the plague
   D. the effects of the plague in London were not particularly severe

22. On the evidence of the passage, which of the following statements best   **22.** ______
describes Pepys's feelings and outlook during the incident?
   A. objective and rational   **C.** sympathetic
   B. proudly indifferent   **D.** suspicious

Read the following passage. Then answer the questions that follow. Write the letter
of the correct answer on the line at the right.

> I saw they had dug several pits in another ground, when the distemper began
> to spread in our parish, and especially when the dead carts began to go about,
> which was not, in our parish, till the beginning of August....But now, at the
> beginning of September, the plague raging in a dreadful manner, and the number
> of burials in our parish increasing to more than was ever buried in any parish
> about London of no larger extent, they ordered this dreadful gulf to be dug, for
> such it was rather than a pit.

[Daniel Defoe, *A Journal of the Plague Year*]

23. Which of the following statements is an opinion presented in the passage?   **23.** ______
   A. The dead carts in the writer's parish first appeared at the beginning of
      August.
   B. The plague raged badly at the beginning of September.
   C. A record number of burials occurred in the writer's parish for a district of
      that size.
   D. To bury the dead, a dreadful gulf, rather than a pit, was dug.

24. Which of the following items best expresses the connotations of the verb *raging* 24. ______
as it is used in the last sentence of the passage?
   A. lack of control   C. suddenly fatal
   B. angry shouting   D. mournful anguish

Read the following passage. Then answer the questions that follow. Write the letter
of the correct answer on the line at the right.

> But great allowances should be given to a king who lives wholly secluded from
> the rest of the world, and must therefore be altogether unacquainted with the
> manners and customs that most prevail in other nations: the want of which
> knowledge will ever produce many prejudices, and a certain narrowness of
> thinking, from which we and the politer countries of Europe are wholly exempted.
> And it would be hard indeed, if so remote a prince's notions of virtue and vice
> were to be offered as a standard for all mankind.

[Jonathan Swift, *Gulliver's Travels*]

25. According to the passage, what is the result of the king's living so far away from 25. ______
the rest of the world?
   A. a lack of knowledge and a certain narrowness of thinking
   B. the necessity of making long journeys to visit other nations
   C. a common outlook with that of the other European nations
   D. a moral code that should serve as the standard for all mankind

26. What is the best synonym for the word *allowances* in the first sentence?   26. ______
   A. excuses or exemptions   C. amounts of money
   B. reductions   D. permissions

27. From the narrator's comments about the king and about the "politer countries 27. ______
of Europe," it seems that the narrator
   A. is convinced that the king's notions about virtue and vice are rather
      primitive
   B. is entirely in agreement with the king's philosophy
   C. has considered the king's arguments fully and fairly
   D. is a spokesman for Swift's own views

Read the following passage. Then answer the questions that follow. Write the letter
of the correct answer on the line at the right.

> **pa' tron.** One who countenances, supports, or protects. Commonly a wretch
> who supports with insolence, and is paid with flattery.

[Samuel Johnson, *A Dictionary of the English Language*]

28. The format of this passage shows that it is drawn from
   A. an atlas   C. a dictionary   28. ______
   B. a magazine article   D. an encyclopedia article

29. The second sentence of this passage is best described as   29. ______
   A. a fact   **C.** an opinion
   B. a nonfact   **D.** a paraphrase

Read the following passage. Then answer the questions that follow. Write the letter of the correct answer on the line at the right.

> Man is, in general, made up of contradictory qualities; and these will ever show themselves in strange succession, where a consistency in appearance, if not in reality, has not been attained by long habits of philosophical discipline. In proportion to the native vigor of the mind, the contradictory qualities will be the more prominent, and more difficult to be adjusted; and, therefore, we are not to wonder that Johnson exhibited an eminent example of this remark which I have made upon human nature. At different times, he seemed a different man, in some respects....

[James Boswell, *The Life of Samuel Johnson*]

30. Which statement below is the best paraphrase of the first sentence?   30. ______
   A. The contradictions in human beings are especially clear in people who have not trained themselves to be consistent.
   B. Inconsistent behavior is to be expected of everyone.
   C. Consistency is not important; contradictions are.
   D. People who cannot behave consistently should be more philosophical.

31. Which of the following most accurately describes the first sentence of the   31. ______
passage?
   A. a metaphor   **C.** a paraphrase
   B. a generalization   **D.** a prejudice

32. On the evidence of this passage, the reader might judge that the author was   32. ______
   A. irritable and impatient   **C.** patient and tolerant
   B. proud and selfish   **D.** materialistic

Read the following passage. Then answer the questions that follow. Write the letter of the correct answer on the line at the right.

> Let not Ambition mock their useful toil,
> Their homely joys, and destiny obscure;
> Nor Grandeur hear with a disdainful smile
> The short and simple annals of the poor.

[Thomas Gray, "Elegy Written in a Country Churchyard"]

33. The descriptions of Ambition and Grandeur in lines 1 and 3 are examples of   33. ______
   A. simile   **C.** personification
   B. metaphor   **D.** overstatement

34. From this passage, you can infer that the speaker   34. _______
   A. lives in the village where the poor people are buried
   B. is angry with those who have paid no attention to the poor
   C. is sympathetic to the simple joys and sorrows of the poor
   D. looks down on the poor

Read the following passage. Then answer the questions that follow. Write the letter of the correct answer on the line at the right.

> The Master said, Govern the people by regulations, keep order among them by chastisements, and they will flee from you and lose all self-respect. Govern them by moral force, keep order among them by ritual, and they will keep their self-respect and come to you of their own accord.

[Confucius, *The Analects*]

35. Which of the following statements best expresses the implied main idea of the   35. _______
   passage?
   A. It is better to rule gently and by example than to govern by imposing orders
      and punishments.
   B. If people will not obey the ruler's orders, they should be punished.
   C. Some people prefer to lead, while others prefer to follow.
   D. Not everyone is born to rule.

Read the following passage. Then answer the questions that follow. Write the letter of the correct answer on the line at the right.

> Home is where the heart is. There's no place like it. I love my home with a ferocity totally out of proportion to its appearance or location. I love dumb things about it: the hot-water heater, the plastic rack you drain dishes in, the roof over my head, which occasionally leaks. And yet it is precisely those dumb things that make it what it is—a place of certainty, stability, predictability, privacy, for me and for my family. It is where I live. What more can you say about a place than that? That is everything.

[Anna Quindlen, "Homeless"]

36. Which sentence gives the main idea of the passage?   36. _______
   A. the first sentence   C. the sixth sentence
   B. the fourth sentence   D. the last sentence

37. Some information in the passage is important and some is unimportant.   37. _______
   Choose the statement below that is *not* important to the main idea of the
   passage.
   A. The writer loves her home ferociously.
   B. The writer loves dumb things about her home.
   C. The writer's home is a place of certainty and stability.
   D. The roof occasionally leaks.

38. What generalization can you make about a person's home, based on this passage?
    A. Some people love their homes more than others.
    B. It takes endurance to live in an old, run-down home.
    C. People often feel extremely attached to their home, whatever its appearance or location.
    D. People will do almost anything to protect their home.

38. ______

Read the following passage. Then answer the questions that follow. Write the letter of the correct answer on the line at the right.

> The people of this country have many origins; these strands are woven together to make us what we are. My own personal background is, perhaps, an illustration. My great great grandfather, William Ellis, was twice Lord Mayor of York in England in 1799 and 1807. My great grandfather arrived in this country as a soldier in the 93rd Sutherland Highlanders regiment in 1803. He married a Clare woman whose mother's name was Morony. Their son settled in Spanish Point in County Clare, my own father's place of origin. My mother, whose family had both Irish and Scottish ancestors, came from Tullamore in County Offaly. My parents spent virtually all their adult life in Dunmurry, near Belfast.
>
> [Judge Catherine McGuinness, "Opening Statement for the Inaugural Session of the Forum for Peace and Reconciliation"]

39. Which of the following sources do you think the writer used for the facts she provides in this passage?
    A. encyclopedia articles   **C.** dictionaries
    B. family records   **D.** interviews

39. ______

40. What object does the metaphor in the first sentence suggest to you?
    A. a warm overcoat
    B. a flag waving in the breeze
    C. a piece of cloth with many colors
    D. a shining star

40. ______

Read the following passage. Then answer the questions that follow. Write the letter of the correct answer on the line at the right.

> The square finger, moving here and there, lighted suddenly on Bitzer, perhaps because he chanced to sit in the same ray of sunlight which, darting in at one of the bare windows of the intensely whitewashed room, irradiated Sissy. For, the boys and girls sat on the face of the inclined plane in two compact bodies, divided up the center by a narrow interval; and Sissy, being at the corner of a row on the sunny side, came in for the beginning of a sunbeam, of which Bitzer, being at the corner of a row on the other side, a few rows in advance, caught the end.
>
> [Charles Dickens, *Hard Times*]

NAME ____ **DATE** ____________

41. From the description in the passage, you can infer that the boys and girls are probably   **41.** ______
    A. in a schoolroom   **C.** at a playground
    B. on a trip to the country   **D.** in a school bus

42. The description shows that Sissy and Bitzer   **42.** ______
    A. are sitting next to each other
    B. are both sitting in the last row
    C. are both sitting at the corner of a row
    D. are sitting one behind the other

Read the following passage. Then answer the questions that follow. Write the letter of the correct answer on the line at the right.

> The partridge of the war zone shows no signs of...sensitive nerves. The rattle and rumble of transport, the constant coming and going of bodies of troops, the incessant rattle of musketry and deafening explosions of artillery, the night-long flare and flicker of star-shells, have not sufficed to scare the local birds away from their chosen feeding grounds, and to all appearances they have not been deterred from raising their broods. Gamekeepers who are serving with the colors might seize the opportunity to indulge in a little useful nature study.

[Saki (H. H. Munro), "Birds on the Western Front"]

43. Which sentence contains the main idea of this passage?   **43.** ______
    A. first sentence   **C.** third sentence
    B. second sentence   **D.** main idea is implied, not stated

44. If the writer were asked his opinion of war, which statement below do you think would best express his answer?   **44.** ______
    A. War is a necessary evil.
    B. War may be justified, but only under certain conditions.
    C. War brings out people's capacity for sacrifice and glory.
    D. War is unnatural and destructive.

45. Which of the following judgments about the overall tone of the passage do you think is most accurate?   **45.** ______
    A. bittersweet and nostalgic   **C.** ironic and satirical
    B. warm and affectionate   **D.** factual and objective

Use this chart to answer the following questions.

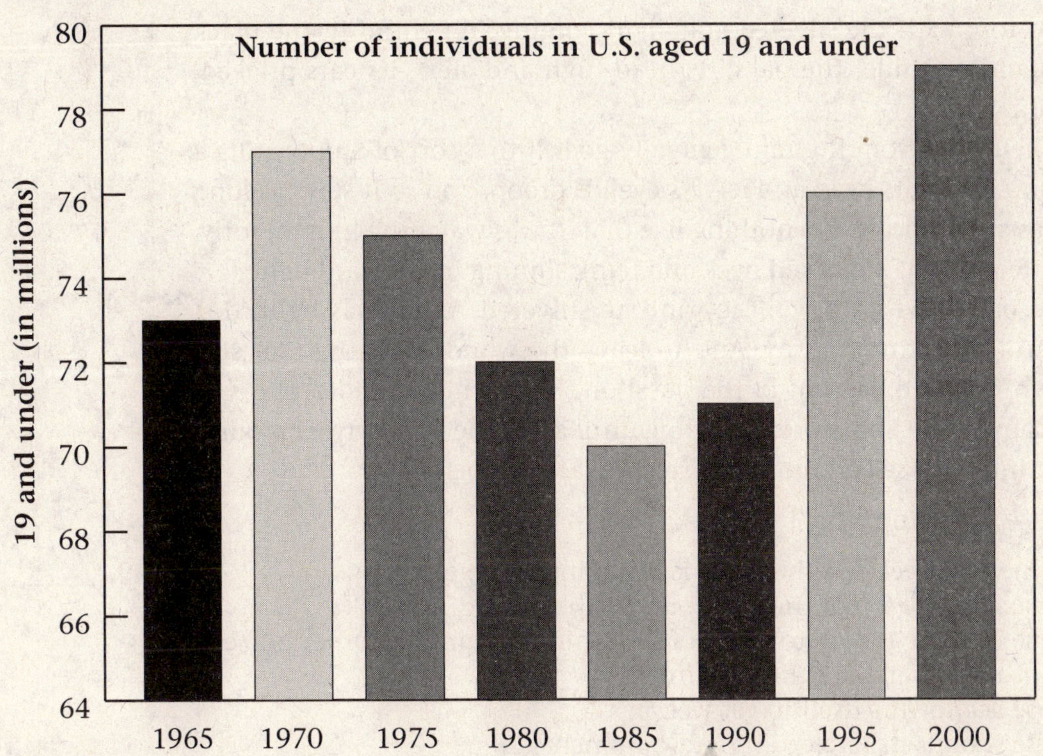

46. According to the graph, when is the population of individuals aged nineteen and under the highest?   46. ______
A. 1970   C. 1995
B. 1990   D. 2000

47. Between 1970 and 1985, the population of individuals who were nineteen years old and under was   47. ______
A. level   C. increasing
B. decreasing   D. decreasing and then increasing

48. In 1980, how many individuals aged nineteen and under were there?   48. ______
A. 70 million   C. 73 million
B. 72 million   D. 80 million

Read the following passage. Then answer the questions that follow. Write the letter of the correct answer on the line at the right.

At the wood top, with the silvered gray light coming in behind it, the black horse was standing under the oaks, its head high and alert, its ears pricked, watching him.

A horse sheltering from the rain generally goes into a sort of stupor, tilts a hind hoof and hangs its head and lets its eyelids droop, and so it stays as long as the rain lasts. This horse was nothing like that. It was watching him intently, standing perfectly still, its soaked neck and flank shining in the hard light.

He turned back. His scalp went icy and he shivered. What was he to do? Ridiculous to try driving it away. And to leave the wood, with the rain still coming down full pelt, was out of the question. Meanwhile the idea of being watched became more and more unsettling until at last he had to twist around again, to see if the horse had moved. It stood exactly as before.

[Ted Hughes, "The Rain Horse"]

49. Why does the man feel that the horse is behaving strangely?   49. ______
    A. The horse is at the top of the wood, under the oaks.
    B. The horse has not gone into a sort of stupor in the rain, like other horses, but seems to be watching the man intently.
    C. The horse is allowing itself to get wet.
    D. The horse stamps its foreleg every few moments.

50. Which statement below best expresses the problem the man faces in this   50. ______
passage?
    A. He does not know the identity of the horse's owner.
    B. He has lost his way in the wood.
    C. He needs to capture the horse but has no idea how to go about it.
    D. The horse makes him uncomfortable, but he does not want to leave the wood because of the driving rain.

